Jeannette & Emanuel
Honig – 1952
11th
February

# THE HOUSE OF COALPORT
## *1750 - 1950*

"THE WILLOW PATTERN"

*Originated in China and introduced in England in 1780 by Thomas Turner*

*" The willow pattern that we knew*
*In childhood, with its bridge of blue*
*Leading to unknown thoroughfares "*

# THE HOUSE OF COALPORT
## 1750-1950

"THE WILLOW PATTERN"

*Originated in China and introduced in England in 1780 by Thomas Turner*

"*The willow pattern that we knew*
*In childhood, with its bridge of blue*
*Leading to unknown thoroughfares*"

# THE HOUSE
# OF
# COALPORT

*1750-1950*

*By*
COMPTON MACKENZIE

COLLINS
ST JAMES'S PLACE, LONDON
1951

PRINTED IN GREAT BRITAIN
COLLINS CLEAR-TYPE PRESS : LONDON AND GLASGOW
COLOUR BLOCKS BY THE FINE ART ENGRAVERS LTD.
1951

*Dedicated
to the workpeople—past and present—
of the Coalport China Company*

# Contents

# *Illustrations*

## COLOUR

# BLACK AND WHITE

# I

## *Caughley*

ON THE high ground above the southern and
westerly banks of the river Severn not far from
Broseley in Shropshire, stands a gamekeeper's
cottage of red brick mellowed by the years. No other
dwellings are in sight, although the main road and the
tiny hamlet of Caughley[1] are but a few hundred yards
away. The view is of undulating fields and woodland
into which the track continues past the cottage to wind
down through the trees toward the hidden river something
over a mile away. No prospect seemingly more remote
from any kind of industrialism could be imagined than
that from the four casements of this lonely cottage. The
only sound audible is the bark of some spaniel or retriever
on guard within, and when the dog is silent, the lowing of
a distant cow and the first bird-song of earliest spring.
Yet that lonely cottage in the middle of the eighteenth
century was a part of " all those erections and buildings
situate standing and being at Caughley aforesaid and used
as a china work and saggar work, with all the workhouses, shops, and appurtenances thereto," to quote in

---

[1] Pronounced " Carfley."

anticipation from an Indenture dated December 1, 1789.

If any doubt lingered of our having discovered the surviving relic of the origins of Coalport China it vanished when we[1] found that the garden of this cottage was still strewn with innumerable fragments of china, mostly blue, all of which must have been turned over by fork or spade, for at least a century and a quarter.

Above the porch between the two casements of the upper storey there is a curious circular cavity in the brickwork which once upon a time was occupied by a clock installed to keep the workmen reminded of time's importance in industry. We shall hear of this clock again. Then we noticed that the soil of a sparsely wooded slope opposite was black. This was evidence of the coal that was once so conveniently dug here for the kilns, and we realised that after all industry had in fact left an indelible scar upon the pastoral scene. We begin to understand why about the year 1750, probably a year or two earlier, Squire Edward Browne of Caughley Hall decided to supplement his agricultural revenue by embarking upon a traditional industry of the neighbourhood, with clay and coal to hand upon his own estate.

In point of fact, we are in the midst of a very old centre of industry.

To quote Llewellynn Jewitt, a connoisseur of china, writing of Coalport in *The Art Journal* of March, 1862 :

Broseley, whose pipe manufactories two hundred and fifty years ago were as famed as they are now, . . . Jackfield, famed of old for its earthenware. . . . Benthall, whose " yellow ware " works are in constant operation, and where the magnificent

[1]We were accompanied on this expedition by Mr. Alfred Langford, the late Art Director of the Coalport China Company, Ltd., whose help was invaluable.

*Sole remaining building (photographed in 1950) of original works at Caughley. The clock, shown on page 121, fitted into the recess between the two top windows*

encaustic and enamelled tile and mosaic works of Messrs. Maw are situated ;—Ironbridge, with its famous one-arch bridge, from which it takes its name, spanning the Severn ;— Madeley, with its extensive iron furnaces. . . . Coalbrookdale, whose iron works are known throughout the world, and where articles in terra-cotta are about being manufactured ; and a score of other busy hives of industry are gathered together in this district, close around the Coalport China Works, whose productions are of unrivalled excellence.

All these places are components of the ancient borough of Wenlock, which in respect of the area it covers is the largest in England, the centre of the civic life being Much Wenlock ; it rivals any little town in England in the beauty and interest of its buildings. In the Guildhall with its oaken panelling within and its sixteenth century black and white without, a remarkable timber structure erected upon the stone buildings of the original prison, may be seen the long roll of the Bailiffs of Wenlock from the Middle Ages until to-day. In 1747 Edward Browne was Bailiff, and we may fancy that the enterprise at Caughley was inspired by his intercourse with the worthies of local industry.

Coalbrookdale, the product of industrialism, is an extraordinarily picturesque village, the houses of which all seem to cling to the hillside above the swift-running brook, and the ironworks founded round about 1740 exhale a kind of gothic romance in the hollow of the wooded dale. From these works presided over by four Abraham Darbys in turn, came the first three-legged iron pot in England, the first iron bridge, and the first iron kettle. There is an agreeable appropriateness in those old tea-kettles from Coalbrookdale and the old tea-pots from Coal-

*The Caughley China Works in 1750 from an engraving published in " The Salopian Monthly Illustrated Journal " of April, 1875*

port being made within four miles of one another. There is still a line of cottages in the former called Tea-Kettle Row.

Between Coalbrookdale and Coalport, on the other side of the Severn from Broseley, Jackfield and Caughley, is Iron-Bridge, as it was originally written, which takes its name from the bridge of the third Abraham Darby. The stone abutments were built in 1777-78 while the ironwork was being cast in open sand. It was then erected in three months and opened for traffic in 1779. The main arch has a span of one hundred feet with a rise of forty-five feet, and it consists of five cast iron ribs, each cast in two portions. The weight of metal in the bridge is about 380 tons. The bridge is closed to-day to all except pedestrians and bicyclists who both pay a toll. Half a mile along on the road to Coalport is the Free Bridge, which was opened for traffic in 1908.

As one stands on the Iron Bridge and looks down upon the turbulent Severn in spate, one asks how long it will be before the " rationalisation " of industry will mean the abandonment of this fair countryside to its own beauty. When almost all that is left of the great city of Uriconium which once covered 170 acres is a fragment of Roman wall in the middle of a field, the cottage at Caughley seems comparatively a larger survival ; but this much Uriconium and Caughley, Broseley, Jackfield and Coalport will have in common : the remote future will find the fragments of their fictile ware when the last kiln has gone the way of the Roman columns. From the fields round Wroxeter the plough may still turn up a potsherd fashioned of the same white clay as that once used in Broseley to make churchwarden pipes. When the barbaric Saxons destroyed Uriconium in A.D. 584 and drove those of its inhabitants they did not massacre to take refuge farther west, they destroyed a great city of whose history we know absolutely nothing during the five centuries that elapsed after Agricola defeated the Ordovices in A.D. 78. Five centuries back from to-day would take us well beyond Bosworth Field where the white rose petals of Merrie England fell faded, and from the blooming of the grafted Tudor rose Modern England was born. During those five centuries of unimaginable civic life the Salopian clay was being kneaded and shaped and baked to provide utensils for the people of Uriconium to drink from, eat from, and cook with. The pots were broken, but the shards endure. The bones of the potter are more perishable than the fragments of his handiwork.

IRONBRIDGE, SHROPSHIRE.
1826

*Design on reverse of mug in memory of Capt. Webb (see page 92).
It shows the celebrated Iron Bridge between Coalbrookdale and
Broseley which was opened for traffic in 1779 and is used to-day
for pedestrians and cyclists*

Forgive this divagation, and let us return to Squire
Browne of Caughley, of whom we do not know very much
more than of a centurion of the Fourteenth Legion in
Uriconium. He died in 1753, his will, made on August
27th, 1749, being proved in the prerogative Court of the
Archbishop of Canterbury on July 19th of that year, by

H.C.                                                      B

which he left all his Estate to his wife, Jane Browne. This date suggests that he had already started his pottery by 1749. She under a will dated 1779 left all her property to Ralph Browne Wylde.

The china works were carried on by a nephew of Edward Browne or his wife called Ambrose Gallimore, who served Much Wenlock as Bailiff in the year 1785. In 1754 Gallimore was granted a lease of the small pottery for a term of sixty-two years ; it was then making an opaque stone china.

The next mention of the Caughley works in a legal deed is in the Indenture already quoted, made between Ralph Browne Wylde and a Thomas Swinnerton of Newcastle-under-Lyme dated December 1st, 1787 : " And also of all those erections and buildings situate standing and being at Caughley aforesaid and used as a china work and saggar work, with all workhouses, shops and appurtenances thereto belonging then in the holding of Thomas Turner and Ambrose Gallimore."

This is the first and last mention of Thomas Swinnerton, and nothing has been found out about his interest in Caughley.

Thomas Turner is a figure of considerably more importance to the beginnings of Coalport china than either Squire Browne or Ambrose Gallimore ; indeed, one can assert that without his influence over the future of Caughley there would never have been any Coalport china.

Thomas Turner was a son of the Reverend Richard Turner, LL.D., Rector of Little Cumberton and Vicar of Elmley Castle, Worcestershire. Dr. Turner took his degree at Magdalen Hall, Oxford, and was the author of several works on trigonometry and astronomy. By 1765 he was

## A Two-Handled Vase

*Partly completed by Charles Walker, one of the victims of the Ferry-Boat disaster in 1799. The illustration is of the one vase showing the design on both its sides*

established as a " Teacher of geometry, astronomy and philosophy at Worcester." He died at Norton-juxta-Kempsey in 1791, and besides Thomas, had two other sons —Richard Turner, author of a very popular *Introduction to Geography*, and General Edward Turner of the Army in India.

Thomas Turner was born in 1749, and at an early age was articled to the Worcester Porcelain Company where he worked, under the tutorship of Robert Hancock, as an engraver of plates for the purpose of transfer. We know that Hancock began to instruct pupils in his art in 1765 and that suggests a probable date for Thomas Turner's start at Worcester, he being then sixteen years of age. The statement that he was apprenticed to a silversmith in Worcester has no basis in fact.

The Worcester Porcelain Company owed its establishment chiefly to the vision of Dr. John Wall, a physician, a chemist and a painter of much ability. In 1772 the Worcester Porcelain Company with all its property was sold by auction for the sum of £5250, and a new company was formed in which Dr. Wall was still the leading figure and in which Robert Hancock held the share that he sold for £900 in 1774.

It seems safe to take 1772 as the year when Thomas Turner came from Worcester to Caughley, but it is tantalising not to be able to find the connecting link between him and Ambrose Gallimore, whom he must have been able to persuade almost at once to begin building the large addition to the factory at Caughley. *Chaffers*[1] says : " Perry, one of the workmen who was apprenticed to Mr.

[1]*Marks and Monograms on European and Oriental Pottery and Porcelain.* With Historical Notices of each Manufactory by William Chaffers. Edited by Frederick Litchfield. (London: William Reeves (Bookseller) Ltd.)

Turner stated that . . . he recollected a slab in front of one
of the arches of the building at Caughley, stating the date
of its foundation, 1772, which would be the time he
succeeded Mr. Gallimore."

*Chaffers* elsewhere presumes that the ownership of the
Caughley works passed at once to Turner, but the
indenture quoted above shows that Turner and Gallimore
were still joint holders in 1787, five years after Turner had
married Gallimore's daughter, Dorothy. What can reason-
ably be presumed is that, within a very short time of his
arrival at Caughley, Turner took on the sole direction of
a business which by 1756 had already developed under
the direction of Gallimore from its earthenware stage.
Llewellynn Jewitt in that article in *The Art Journal* already
quoted says : " In 1756 the works had attained a considerable degree of excellence ; and an example is in
existence, bearing that date, which gives most satisfactory
evidence of the excellence of the body at that time—a
body, however, which speedily became greatly improved."

At this point the attention of the reader is directed to
the engraving of the old Caughley works. The new
building with the arches is in the middle. On the extreme
left is the gamekeeper's cottage of to-day with the clock
in its place. That clock dated 1799, went to Coalport
when the works, except for that one piece of the building,
were removed there brick by brick in 1814-15. That
clock accompanied the move from Coalport to Shelton in
1925, and it is at the Crescent works in Stoke-upon-Trent
to-day.

The building of the additional works begun in 1772 was
finished in 1775. A newspaper paragraph of that year
announces :

The porcelain manufactory erected near Bridgnorth, in this county, is now quite completed, and the proprietors have received and supplied orders to a very large amount. Lately we saw some of their productions which in colour and fineness are truly elegant and beautiful, and have the bright and lively white of the so much extolled Oriental.

The best known example of this period is a white mug with blue and gold flowers and inscribed *Francis Benbow, 1776* beneath an anchor to mark the owner's profession as a bargeman.

*Chaffers* says :

Robert Hancock, the artist-engraver of better known Worcester fame, is said to have worked with Turner some time after 1774, and is probably responsible for the good transfer decoration in blue under glaze which we find occasionally on some good Caughley specimens.

John Randall in *The Clay Industries on the Banks of the Severn* published at Madeley in 1877 says :

Printing on porcelain appears first to have been introduced by Dr. Wall at the Worcester Works, a process soon after taken to Caughley by a person named Holdship, a former painter in the Worcester Works, where it was practised as a great secret, with closed doors, as at Caughley.

Whether either Holdship or Hancock joined Turner at Caughley is not absolutely certain, though it is known that Hancock left the new Worcester Porcelain Company in 1774 after a quarrel with the other partners and as the tutor of Turner in Worcester he may have joined his old pupil for a while.

There were two Holdships, Richard and Josiah, and each held a twentieth share in the original Worcester

Porcelain Company. Richard went bankrupt in 1761 and departed to work in Derby, where he agreed to paint for Duesbury who had founded the Derby Porcelain Works in 1756. The Editor of *Chaffers*, judging from the only specimen of Holdship's work for Derby he had seen, declared that " the experiment was not a success."

Richard's younger brother, Josiah, would also seem to have been less accomplished than he pretended to be if we may judge from a couplet in Berrow's *Worcester Journal* of December, 1757 :

> *Hancock, my friend, don't grieve, tho' Holdship has the praise,*
> *'Tis yours to execute, 'tis his to wear the bays.*

However, in the following month, January, 1758, the *Worcester Journal* was acclaiming Josiah Holdship in verse as the perfecter of the art of painting on porcelain :

> What praise is thine, ingenious Holdship ! who
> On the fair porcelain the portrait drew,
> To thee, who first, in thy judicious mind,
> A perfect model of the art designed,
> An art which, long by curious artists sought,
> By thee alone to great perfection's brought.

Nevertheless, in spite of this encomium, it does not look as if the two Holdships contributed much to the development of painting on porcelain.

Jewitt writes :

The subject of printing upon porcelain, of which I have spoken in previous articles, is one so intimately and intricately connected with the Caughley and Coalport works, that it will be necessary to consider the period of its introduction at some length. I have already shown that transfer-printing was used as early as 1757 on Worcester porcelain ; and I have little doubt that quite as early, if not a few years before that period, it was practised at Caughley. Indeed, in the early years of the manufactory, the two works, Caughley and Worcester, seem to have been closely connected, and to have worked " in-and-in," if I may be allowed the use of so unscientific an expression, and, I believe, with ample reason, that a great proportion of the printed goods bearing the Worcester mark were printed at Caughley. Indeed, it is known that the ware was sent up from Worcester by barge to be printed at Caughley, and returned, when finished, by the same mode of conveyance. I have closely examined the style of engraving, and the patterns of a large number of examples, and I am clearly of opinion that they are the work of the same hands.

I do not, by this, claim for Caughley the honour of inventing the art of transfer-printing on to porcelain ; but I feel assured, that that art must have been there practised at quite as early a period as the dated example of Worcester make ; and I am led to this belief, partly from the fact that the Robert Hancock, whose beautiful productions I have before spoken of, and to whom the engraving of the dated example is ascribed, also engraved for the Caughley works. And I have an impression of a plate, of an identical pattern with the famous tea group, which bears his monogram on the Worcester specimens, on which his name, *R. Hancock fecit*, occurs in full at Caughley. Collectors, therefore, in a case of this kind must not be too hasty in ascribing, from appearance alone, examples to either one or the other make, but must be guided, in a great measure, by the body on which the engraving occurs.

It cannot be wondered that an art, then such an important secret, should have been followed at Caughley,—a place so perfectly retired from the world, situated in the midst of woods and wilds, almost unapproachable to strangers, and with every facility for keeping the workmen away from all chance of imparting the secret to others,—in place of Worcester, where secrecy would be almost impossible, and where the information would ooze out from the workmen, at the alehouse or elsewhere, and be greedily caught up by those interested in the process. At Caughley every possible precaution seems to have been taken to secure secrecy ; and the workmen—the engravers and printers—were locked up and kept apart from every one else. Who the engravers were, I cannot satisfactorily say. It is, however, certain that Hancock engraved for the works : and it is said that Holdship, of whom I have before spoken, was also employed. Among the other engravers was a man named Dyas, who was apprenticed as an engraver at Caughley, about the year 1768, and who continued at the works until his death, at the ripe age of eighty-two. It is also worthy of note that Mr. Minton, the father of Mr. Herbert Minton, was also apprenticed as an engraver at these works. It is not too much to say, that the style of engraving adopted at so early a period was remarkably good, and of really high character. Indeed, some specimens which I have seen of the plates used at Caughley, are far superior to most of the productions of the period.

In 1896 the Editor of *Chaffers* visited R. W. Binns, the " veteran director " of the Worcester Porcelain Works, and to him Binns declared that *Chaffers* was wrong in calling Richard Holdship an engraver, adding that in fact he was a glover and his brother Josiah a maltster. He said that Josiah Holdship " evidently appreciated the engraving of Hancock and took the credit to himself . . . it is said that when he (Hancock) left, there was a dispute about the copper-plates, which might easily have arisen if he claimed the copyright, the other partners, probably at Holdship's suggestion, endeavouring to take the credit of their excellence for themselves. The fact may also have

"THE INDIAN TREE"

*Originated 1801*

given colour to the assertion of the late Mr. Llewellynn Jewitt, who found some few of Hancock's copper-plates at Coalport."

It seems reasonable to speculate that Thomas Turner acquired some of the copper-plates of his old master, but there is no evidence for Richard's or Josiah Holdship's being loaned to Caughley to betray a secret process. Moreover, one must suppose that Turner during the seven years he was working at Worcester would have reached Caughley, equipped with the secrets himself, and his cordial relations with Worcester which will be noted presently do not suggest any underhand business.

About the year 1780, Turner visited France for the purpose of obtaining information about the porcelain manufacturers of Paris and elsewhere. Being an excellent draughtsman himself and a skilled chemist, with a private laboratory he had fitted out on the top floor of the house he rented in France, Turner was able to learn a lot, and one may surmise that the dark blue of the Caughley china was one fruit of this visit to France. Moreover, he brought back with him some skilled French artists and workmen. During the next decade among those engaged at Caughley were Dontil, a painter, and De Vivy, a modeller. In England he found John Parker, Henry Boden, and Thomas Fennel for flowers, Thomas Martin Randall for birds, his brother Edward Randall for gilding, Adams for a painter in blue and Muss and Silk for landscapes. Muss later went to London and enjoyed much success as a landscape painter. There was also Stephen, a German modeller, whose son Peter was for a long time modeller at Coalport. John Rose, the son of an *emigré*

Scottish farmer in the neighbourhood, was articled to Turner, whom he left after a quarrel about the time the latter went to France, to start a small business of his own in Jackfield. We shall hear a great deal more about John Rose in due course. Of Thomas Martin Randall and his brother we shall also hear more.

Not only did Turner bring back with him French artists and workmen familiar with the *turquin* and the *turquoise*, the *bleu du Roi* and *bleu lapis* of Royal Sèvres. He also brought back a French architect who designed for him a *château* which was erected near the works and called Caughley Place. His partner, Ambrose Gallimore, was living in Squire Browne's old house, Caughley Hall. Soon after Caughley Place had impressed the countryside, Turner in 1783 married Dorothy Gallimore, the daughter of his partner. How far this was a *mariage de convenance* suggested by his visit to France does not transpire from any information available. *Chaffers* says that Miss Dorothy Gallimore was a niece of Squire Browne and that she was residing at the time at Caughley Hall ; but if she was a daughter of Ambrose Gallimore she must have been living at Caughley Hall most of her life. Perhaps *Chaffers* is wrong in making 1783 the date of the marriage : perhaps it was much earlier. Elsewhere it writes of Turner that " having married a lady of some property he went to Caughley and began to build suitable premises for the manufacture of porcelain."

There was a legend in the neighbourhood given the currency of the printed word by J. F. Blacker in *Nineteenth Century Ceramic Art* that Thomas Turner had visited Caughley when he was still under articles to the Worcester Porcelain Company, and that falling in love with Ambrose

"Z605"

*Originated 1896*

Gallimore's daughter he had married her, which was the reason he was taken into partnership by his father-in-law. Blacker goes so far as to say it was falling in love with Dorothy Gallimore which made him turn from silver to china. We know that to be wrong, and on the whole we shall be wise to accept *Chaffers'* date for the marriage as 1783, and discount its contradictory information about marrying a lady of some property.

The fact is that *Chaffers* was too much concerned with its erudition about pottery and porcelain to be more than casually interested in domestic details of those that made them. Anyway, Turner's first wife died in 1793 and both the two children of the marriage died young. In 1796 he married Mary Milner, the widow of Henry Alsop, by whom he had two children : Catherine Georgina Cecilia, who married John Jacob Smith (sometime town-clerk of Bridgnorth for fifty years) and died in 1836, and George Thomas Turner, a solicitor, who died at Scarborough in 1869 without issue.

*Chaffers* says :

The excellence of Turner's porcelain, and the invention of the beautiful dark blue of the Caughley china, attributed to him, gained him great patronage. In 1780 he introduced the celebrated Willow Pattern, which even at the present day is in great demand, and the Blue Dragon, another favourite pattern, and completed the first *blue printed table service* made in England for Thomas Whitmore, Esq., of Apsley Park, near Bridgnorth, the pattern was called Nankin, and was something similar to the Broseley tea service produced in 1782, all in porcelain. Mr. Thomas Minton of Stoke assisted in the completion of this service, being then articled as an engraver at Caughley. These two patterns remained universal favourites for many years ; the Willow Pattern for dinner services, and the Broseley for tea and breakfast sets ; they were indispensable in all domestic establishments for ordinary use, and remained so almost exclusively for nearly half a century.

Elsewhere *Chaffers* notes that the original Willow Pattern plate is to be seen in the Portsmouth Museum, having been brought over in H.M.S. *Lion*, the flagship of Lord Macartney's famous embassy to China in 1792, and that it was from this plate that the Staffordshire potters first copied this pattern. If that be true the Willow Pattern can hardly have appeared before 1795 because the embassy did not return to this country until September, 1794.

This plate may have been an inspiration to the Staffordshire potters, but Thomas Turner undoubtedly brought back the Willow Pattern from France, where he may have been given the oriental plates on which it was based. These, according to S. Shaw in his *Staffordshire Potteries* published in 1829, were still in existence when he wrote. The Jesuit missionaries in China were always active practically as well as spiritually. Even the *Concise Oxford Dictionary* finds space to record that *Willow Pattern* is a conventional design of Chinese type done in blue on white china introduced in England in 1780. So let us deprive Lord Macartney of the claim made for his embassy and salute Thomas Turner as the benefactor who has stirred the imagination of countless children, inspiring Longfellow to write :

> *The willow pattern that we knew*
> *In childhood, with its bridge of blue*
> *Leading to unknown thoroughfares.*

There will never be a design so popular as the Willow Pattern. Let everybody make up his own story for it ; the story about the mandarin and his eloping daughter adds no mystery to the bewitching scene.

Blacker writes :

> From the date of its first production at Caughley, it must have appeared upon millions of plates and dishes, cups and saucers, which have been distributed all over the world. I saw a collection of Willow Pattern dishes a short time since, which had been picked up in the towns and villages of the Straits Settlements. Probably it would be difficult to find any inhabited spot on the earth's surface, where an Englishman had lived, without some evidences of the Willow Pattern plate. Many factories have produced it, and successfully. It is not misplaced upon the tables of the rich ; it is welcomed by the poor.

Let it be added as a postscript that Cardinal Newman once picked up half a Willow Pattern saucer in the crater of Vesuvius.

Thomas Minton, a native of Shropshire, mentioned as the engraver who assisted in the service made for Squire Whitmore of Apsley Hall, was articled to Thomas Turner as an engraver, and when his term of service had expired he went to work for Josiah Spode of Stoke-upon-Trent at his London house in Lincoln's Inn Fields. Spode introduced the blue printed old Willow Pattern to Stoke about 1784, which further contradicts the Macartney legend. Thomas Minton came to Stoke in 1788 and in 1790 entered into partnership with Joseph Poulson, who had been manager at Spode's works, to found the famous firm of Minton's.

Jewitt's phrase about the way the two works, Caughley and Worcester, worked " in-and-in " did not apply merely to Worcester wares being sent up by barge to be printed at Caughley, where in 1797 there were four printing presses, introduced there by William Davis, a prominent partner in the Worcester Porcelain Company and sometime manager. The authority for this statement is Perry, an apprentice at Caughley before Thomas Turner came there, who remained on for many years as a workman. He added that the patterns at that date, as they had been for years previously, were birds and blue panels.

When Robert Chamberlain, the first apprentice of the Worcester Porcelain Company, opened a business of his own in partnership with his brother Humphrey in 1786, the new firm obtained their porcelain in the white from Caughley during the next four years. Chamberlains at first were decorators only, and Turner besides supplying them with porcelain in the white used to send large quantities of his own ware to be decorated by them and returned for his own trade. *Chaffers* says that at first Thomas Turner mixed all the bodies himself, but that later he taught his sister how to do it, and that later still a man called Jones mixed for him. This brief glance at Miss Turner is tantalising ; one would like to know more about this competent and active lady, so much in advance of her time. How welcome would have been a sketch of her in one of Miss Austen's letters to her sister Cassandra ! Hubert Smith, the only grandson of Thomas Turner, supplied *Chaffers* with this information. He had portraits of Thomas Turner, Dorothy Turner, Ambrose Gallimore and possibly of the elusive Miss Turner. Where are they now ?

And is the puzzle jug with three spouts which inspired a paragraph by Llewellynn Jewitt in *The Reliquary, Quarterly Archæological Journal and Review*, for January, 1875, still whole? Turner's grandson, Hubert Smith, drew the expert's attention to it. It was eight inches high and formed of the usual body of The Salopian China Warehouse as the Caughley works were styled. It was decorated with blue sprigs and bore on its front within an oval border the name of

IOHN GEARY

CLEAK OF THE

OLD CHURCH

BROSLEY

1789

under which in blue was written "Matthew th V & 16." The substitution of " a " for " r " in the calling of John Geary is as puzzling as the spouts, and even more puzzling is the quotation from the Gospel. " Let your light so shine before men that they may see your good works."

In 1798 or 1799 Thomas Turner retired from business, and the Caughley works were sold to his former apprentice,

*Curious Puzzle Jug of Caughley China, 1789*

John Rose, now established at Coalport. Turner lived on for another ten years in the *château* he had built for himself, and died in 1809 at the age of sixty.

Thomas Turner was undoubtedly a most remarkable man of diverse gifts, and for over a quarter of a century his influence upon the development of English porcelain was profound. Not only was he a complete master of the various processes connected with porcelain manufacture, a skilled chemist, a fine draughtsman, designer and engraver, but he was also an admirable musician. He was a freeman of Worcester, Much Wenlock, and Bridgnorth, and a J.P. for Shropshire and Staffordshire. His taste and discernment, his energy, his ability to choose good workmen and his understanding of what his customers wanted are evident, but it is much to be regretted that we do not possess any impression of his personality from a contemporary student of mankind. He is, indeed, almost as remote as one of the figures in his own enchanting Willow Pattern, and we would fain know more in his case of what Byron called ' the precious porcelain of human clay.' Not even do we possess any notion of what his *château* was like ; John Rose pulled that down in 1820.

" Tantallon Castle "

*Handpainted by Mr. Percy Simpson in 1907*

# II

## Coalport Under the Roses

WE NOW come to the career of another remarkable man. Κεραμεὺς κεραμεῖ κοτέει, wrote Hesiod,
potter cannot agree with potter ; we might add,
when both potters are men of strong personality. The
cause of the difference between Thomas Turner and John
Rose which led to the latter's leaving Caughley and
starting a small business on his own account, was considered by Jewitt irrelevant to his account of Coalport and
there is no chance now of finding out what it was. It is
exasperating to be told that Jewitt knew and failed to
transmit that knowledge. Anyway, according to *Chaffers*,
about the time that Turner went on that fruitful visit to
France, John Rose went to Jackfield to begin on his own.
We are handicapped by more recklessness about dates.
Randall in *The Clay Industries on the Banks of the Severn* says that
John Rose and his brother Thomas were the sons of John
Rose, a Scottish farmer who came down from Scotland
about 1770 and took Swynney Farm, near Broseley. He
goes on to say that John Rose Junior was born February
8th, 1772, and was a clerk with Turner. He would have
been a pretty precocious clerk to be able to leave his

JOHN ROSE (1772-1841)

"*He was founder of the China Manufactory at Coalport and died beloved and respected of all who knew him*"

master about 1780 and start a business of his own—a clerical prodigy indeed. *Chaffers* and Jewitt are both definite about the date of his departure, and Jewitt, who was using information supplied by Hubert Smith, Turner's only grandson, adds that John Rose, " whose father was a farmer in the neighbourhood, was taken into the house by Mr. Turner, and taught the art of china-making in all its branches." Obviously Randall is a good many years out with the date of John Rose's birth, who must have been at least in his early twenties when he went to Jackfield.

Jackfield lies on the bank of the Severn below Caughley and opposite Coalport. The pottery there was believed to have been worked for centuries, and as early as 1560 the parish registers of Stoke-upon-Trent mention people from Jackfield, who were obviously potters, migrating into Staffordshire. In the middle of the nineteenth century, an old coal-pit at Jackfield which had not been entered for nearly two hundred years was opened, and in it was found a small mug of brown earthenware dated 1634. About that date the works were being carried on by one Glover, who used the old salt glaze for his ware. Later about 1713 John Thursfield took over the Jackfield Pottery. He married the daughter of Captain Webb, one of Marlborough's veterans and an ancestor of the Captain Matthew Webb who was the first man to swim the Channel, and also of the husband of Mary Webb, the Shropshire novelist. Thursfield died in 1751 leaving two sons—John who built the Benthal works, and Maurice who succeeded his father at Jackfield. The ware made at Jackfield was a white stoneware similar to the Staffordshire make, but Maurice Thursfield produced a superior black ware, so highly vitrified and glazed that it resembled glass and was known locally as " black decanters." Raised ornamentation in gold and colour was frequently used and on some of the " decanters " views and portraits were painted in oils.

Maurice Thursfield died in America, where he had built up a large business connection, foreshadowing the great business connection with America that Coalport would one day build up.

It was in these works that John Rose, in partnership with a Mr. Blakeway, began making china soon after the death of Maurice Thursfield.

It is not certain how long John Rose remained at Jackfield, but it was not long before the works were removed to Coalport on the other side of the river, where they began in some buildings which had formerly been a pottery belonging to a Shrewsbury mercer called Young. John Rose had not been long established at Coalport in partnership with Blakeway when an opposition business was started by his own brother, Thomas Rose, who arrived with two partners called Anstice and Horton to start works on the other side of the canal only a few yards from " Messrs. John Rose and Company." The rivals did not flourish and within a short while they were absorbed by John Rose, whose Coalport china works prospered to such an extent that the Caughley works began to lose more and more business. This no doubt was why Thomas Turner accepted John Rose's offer to buy the Salopian China Warehouse.

The Coalport china works continued for about fifteen years to make china at Caughley, but it was made there almost entirely in the biscuit state and taken to Coalport to be decorated. John Rose had got together a fine staff

*The remains of the original factory at Coalport. This photograph was taken in 1950*

of workers from Caughley and Jackfield, many of whom lived in Broseley and crossed the Severn twice daily by ferry at a spot called the Tuckies, where the river flows very rapidly. On October 23rd, 1799, when the great stream was in spate after the autumnal rains, the ferryboat, crowded with forty-one of the Coalport workpeople, capsized, and twenty-eight of them were drowned. The nine o'clock bell which signalled the end of that long day's work once upon a time had rung, and in their eagerness to be homeward bound on this cold dark night the passengers may have bestowed themselves aboard without care for the trimming of the boat. According to one account the ferryman, new to the job and drunk, allowed his craft to swing round in the swollen mid-stream, where it was drawn under by the rope which went from the mast to a rock in the bed of the river, and although some of the passengers managed to scramble out on the Broseley side, fifteen women and thirteen men were drowned.

Another account published in *The Shropshire Gazeteer* in 1824 said :

> It was the opinion of those who were preserved that this melancholy accident was caused by the premeditated act of the boatman, who having been some time before refused admittance to a dance given by the persons who were in the daily habit of crossing the stream had expressed his determination *to give them a ducking*. Very probably it was his design merely to frighten those who had offended him, without doing them any real injury. How painful must have been his feelings at the unexpected result of his dangerous frolic ! It becomes us in the midst of sport to beware lest we scatter death.

So fast was the stream flowing that many of the bodies

were found next morning at a great distance from the
Tuckies ; some remained in the water for a month, and
some were never found.

*The Shropshire Gazeteer* was deeply impressed by the
behaviour of " John Rose, Esq."

> The generous master of those who perished provided coffins
> at his own expense for their interment, and was frequently
> seen to shed tears. His benevolent conduct towards the
> surviving sufferers will never be forgotten. It will ever endear
> him in the estimation of his servants, and of the world at large,
> and when he shall be no more, his memory will be held in
> veneration, both as a master and as a friend.

John Rose lost some of his best artists on that night,
among others Charles Walker, who up to within a few
minutes of losing his life was painting a two-handled
vase. This unfinished piece of work was preserved in the
warehouse for nearly 150 years and is a treasured possession
of the present owners.

The tragedy was related in verse by Edward Dyas, who
was then working at Coalport as an engraver. The
original printed version appears on the following page ;
the verse itself is reprinted on page 122. Dyas had
been an apprentice at Caughley as early as 1768. Later
he set up as a painter in Madeley, of which place he
became parish clerk, and here by the accident of upsetting
a glue-pot he started something which revolutionised
printing. Not having a pelt ball or dabber at hand, he
took a piece of glue in a soft state and inked a forme with
it, adding treacle to keep it soft. This led to the development of the printer's roller already invented by Lord
Stanhope without the discovery of a suitable composition
until Dyas upset that glue-pot.

# DREADFUL CALAMITY

WHICH HAPPENED

## AT COALPORT, IN THE PARISH OF MADELEY, SALOP,

*On Wednesday Night, October 23rd, 1799.*

---

The following are the names of the unfortunate persons who were drowned :—

*Jane, Sarah, and Ann Burns, Mary Burgess, Elizabeth and Mary Fletcher, Elizabeth Beard, Elizabeth Ward, Jane Boden, Sarah Bagnal, Sophia Banks, Mary Miles, Elizabeth Evans, Catherine Lowe, Jane Leigh.——Charles Walker, George Lynn, James Arnsworth, George Sheat, John Cheil, Robert Lowe, William Beard, John Jones, Benjamin Gosnal, Benjamin Wyld, Richard Mountford, John Leigh, and Joseph Poole.*

ALAS! alas! the fated night,
  Of cold October's twenty third,
In seventeen hundred ninety nine,
  What cries! what lamentations heard!
The hour nine, when from yon pile,
  Where fair porcelain takes her forms;
Where Energy with Genius joins
  To robe her in those matchless charms;—
A wearied band of artists rose,
  Males and females old and young,
Their toils suspend to seek repose,
  Their homes to gain they bent along.
Sabrina's stream was near to pass
  And she her frowning waves uprear'd;
Her mist condensed to darksome haze,
  Which mock'd the light, no star appear'd.
Yon boat, which o'er her bosom rides,
  Envelop'd in the heavy gloom,
Convulsive stretch'd along her side,
  To snatch the victims to their doom
Soon o'er on board the fatal ring bark,
  A monster fell! who grasp'd the helm,
Hove from the shore the destin'd crew,
  And lo! the dreadful overwhelm!
Swift Horror's wings o'erspread the tide,
  They sink! they rise! they shriek! they cling!
Again they sink! alarm swift flies!
  Along the shores dread clamours ring!
But O! the blackest night preventing
  Every means to save their breath;
Helpless—hopeless—life despairing—
  Twenty-eight sunk down in death!!
Alas! small time for heaven implorings—
  Quick sealed their everlasting state—
Or in misery—or in glory—
  The last tribunal will relate.
Here fold, O Muse, thy feeble wings,
  Hope where thou can'st—but not decide:
Dare not approach those hidden things,
  With Mercy—Justice—they abide.
Return with sympathetic breath,
  See yon distracted mother stands!
Three daughters lost! to heaven she lifts
  Her streaming eyes and wringing hands.
Hark! from those dells how deep the wailing!
  Fathers, mothers, join their moans!
Widows, orphans, friends, and lovers
  Swell the air with poignant groans!
Recluse in grief those worthy masters
  Silent drop the mournful tear:

Distress pervades surrounding hamlets,
  Sorrow weeps to every ear.
Sleepless sighings hail the morning
  Morning brings no soothing ray;
The turbid waters not admitting
  Sight to where the bodies lay.
See them now in strict researches,
  Pierce and drag the river's bed,
Eddys, fords, and rocks imploring
  To give up their silent dead.
Now one, and now another's found,
  And rescued from the wasting waves;
Reviving griefs attend arround,
  And pity bears them to their graves.
How great the loss of shining artists!
  How desponding in their end!
How deeply felt the gone support
  Of children, fathers, mothers, friends!
O ye, bereft of earthly comfort,
  Seek it from the realms above.
God gave the life, he takes away,
  Tax not his mercy or his love:
Make him your friend by supplication,—
  Tell him your despairing grief,—
Ask the power of true submission,—
  And beg the balm of heaven's relief.
And ye who foiled the jaws of death, *
  Ye, whom that vent'ring hero saved, †
Ye, who escap'd that vengeful hour, ‡
  In which your comrades were enwaved:—
Will you no ardent praises raise,
  To Him, by whose supreme controul
The elements give life or death,
  In vengeance or in mercy roll?
Will you those just commands deride,
  Which bid you fear and love your God!—
His sabbaths keep—His precepts own—
  And bend your steps to his abode?
Will you in Satan's cause combine,
  And run in hell's destructive race?
Will you the scorn'd and scorner join,
  And spit in tender Mercy's face?
Forbid it reason's pleading voice.—
  Forbid all ye powers above,
Forbid it truth's celestial ray,—
  Forbid it gratitude and love.
O let your lengthen'd hours proclaim
  The sparing mercies of your God;
Walk humbly with him all your days—
  Revere his goodness—dread his rod.

---

* Thirteen men, women, and children, who got safe to shore.   † Edward Parker, an excellent swimmer, fetched off two boys, who clung to the boat.   ‡ Several persons who used to go over at that hour but by some unseen Providence had left work at six o'clock.

IRONBRIDGE: WALTER, PRINTER, HIGH STREET.

Dyas is obscure on the exact cause of the disaster. He seems to suggest that a demon took charge of the helm, perhaps with the intention of implying a Satanic inspiration for the ferryman.

As time went on the coal at Caughley began to show signs of approaching exhaustion, and the expense of transporting the unfinished ware down the hill and over the river to Coalport was uneconomic even at the low price paid to the women, who carried it the whole way on their heads. Rose made up his mind to concentrate gradually at Coalport. It should be noted that Gallimore's original lease for sixty-two years made in 1754 would be expiring in 1816 and we have no information of its having been extended. In 1814 the last workmen were removed to Coalport from Caughley, the kilns and buildings were taken down, and the materials were used to enlarge the works at Coalport. Turner's *château* was the last to be taken down. That was in 1821 when the substance of Caughley Place was removed to build burnishing shops and workmen's cottages at Coalport. Caughley Hall was pulled down as well as Caughley Place, but there is no record to say that the bricks of Caughley Hall went to Coalport ; it seems more probable that they were used in the more immediate neighbourhood. No memorial of Thomas Turner's art and industry was left except that corner of it which to-day is a lonely gamekeeper's cottage whose windows look out upon the blackened soil, all that remains of the coal, and whose garden is strewn with chips of blue and white porcelain, all that remains of The Salopian China Warehouse.

In 1820, John Rose and Company of Coalport bought the Swansea works and entered into an agreement with

Billingsley and his son-in-law, Samuel Walker, to make for Coalport the superior kind of porcelain which William Billingsley and Walker had been making first at Nantgarw in Glamorganshire and afterwards at the Cambrian Pottery of Swansea.

William Billingsley was a great figure in the history of English china. He was born at Derby in 1758; in 1774 at the age of sixteen he was apprenticed to Duesbury of Derby for five years " to be taught the art of painting upon china or porcelain ware " at 5s. a week for the whole of his time. He remained in Derby until 1796, when he joined John Coke in establishing a manufactory at Pinxton. In 1800 Billingsley left Pinxton, taking with him the recipe for mixing his ingredients which he kept a secret until his death; it then came into the hands of John Rose of Coalport. After leaving Pinxton, Billingsley started a small pottery in Mansfield with some of the workmen from Pinxton he had persuaded to accompany him. The venture was not a success, and three years later he started another small pottery at Torksey near Gainsborough : Samuel Walker joined him here and some years later married his daughter. Torksey proved a failure; by 1808 Billingsley was seriously involved financially and for some time travelled about under an assumed name until finally he and Walker were engaged by Flight and Barr of Worcester, where Walker introduced a system of firing called reverberating kilns which was new to Worcester, though already in use at Derby. Walker kept the method of construction a secret and always used to work at night to finish a kiln.

In 1813 Billingsley broke his engagement with Flight and Barr, and quitting Worcester, he and his son-in-law

"THE ARISTOCRAT"

*Originated 1938 as "Democrat"*

started to make porcelain at Nantgarw on the banks of the
Glamorgan canal in the Taff Valley. Their capital soon
ran out ; they borrowed more ; that ran out too ; finally
they made an agreement with Dillwyn, the proprietor of
the Swansea pottery, to work for him. While experiments
were being made, Dillwyn received a letter from Flight
and Barr that " the parties calling themselves Beeley
and Walker had clandestinely left their engagement at
Worcester " and injuncting Dillwyn against employing
them. So Beeley, as he was now called, and Walker
went back to Nantgarw, and two years later in 1820,
after having had to give up the struggle in Nantgarw,
they entered into an arrangement with John Rose, who
bought their stock and plant, to work for him at Coalport.
Billingsley and Walker worked with John Rose until the
former died in 1828, when his son-in-law went to America.
Thus, to quote Jewitt, " one of the most remarkable men
in the whole line of English potters passed away in complete
obscurity, and in much greater poverty than his talents
deserved." Samuel Walker, too, was highly skilled. He
introduced a maroon-ground for Coalport china which
was immensely popular, and it is said that the pottery he
established in America was highly successful.

Before giving an account of Billingsley's secret paste it
will be convenient to speak of another potter who started
with Thomas Turner at Caughley. Thomas Martin
Randall went on from Caughley to Derby and from there
to Pinxton. Then he and another enameller called Robins
started a business in Spa Fields, Islington, where, using
Nantgarw white china, they decorated it in the style of
Sèvres ; this was marketed by Mortlocks, the Oxford
Street china dealers. Randall, a Quaker, refused to forge

the Sèvres mark, but he was able to counterfeit the quality of Sèvres colouring and ornamental patterns so skilfully that to this day the public and private collections of our country contain many doubtful specimens which can be attributed to Randall.

In 1826 Robins and Randall dissolved partnership, and Randall started a china manufactory at Madeley where he turned out beautiful china with a body much resembling that of Nantgarw and Sèvres. However, his paste was very costly and in the firing sometimes the whole contents of a kiln would melt.

Randall died in 1859.

An obituary notice in the *Gentlemen's Magazine* for October of that year says :

> At Shallowford, in the Quakers' burying ground . . . were laid the last remains of a good and clever man. Born at Broseley he served his time at Caughley, the earliest of our Shropshire porcelain works, and the nursery of a class of very clever men. From thence he removed to Coalport, thence to London, afterwards to Madeley, and thence to the Potteries, where he succeeded . . . in producing specimens of porcelain, equal to those he made his model—the highest productions of the Royal Sèvres works in the palmy days of Louis XV. " Ay, sir," said a well-known dealer in the Strand in our hearing, " the old Quaker stands first, at the top of the tree, but he will not put the French mark on his ware, or I could sell any quantity at the tip-top price old Sèvres China sells for." . . . His nephew, John Randall, is at present engaged at the Coalport works as an artist.

This was the John Randall who wrote *The Clay Industries on the Banks of the Severn*, which was published at Madeley in 1877. John Randall lived to a great age,

*The bi-centenary plate modelled by Mr. S. Sanders. The embossment on the rim incorporates the names of "Coalbrookdale," "Broseley," "Caughley," "Swansea," "Nantgarw," "Coalport." Dated 1750 and 1950*

not dying until well into the present century in his late nineties.

It seems likely that Randall learned how to make his Madeley paste from Billingsley, or perhaps " discovered " might be a more appropriate word. This paste of Billingsley's was superior to anything of the kind hitherto produced in England, and could challenge the *pâte tendre* of Sèvres at its best period. It seems that Billingsley perfected his paste in 1813, the year in which he broke his engagement with Flight and Barr at Worcester. John Randall says :

> He produced a fret body by mixing the materials, firing them in order to blend them together, then reducing the vitrified substance into clay—a process which was carried on at old Sèvres during the reign of Louis XV—and thereby produced an article fine in texture, beautifully transparent, and of a delicate waxy hue, very superior to the dingy blue given to much of the best china of that day.

Billingsley's product attracted connoisseurs, and when Mortlock made an agreement to buy all the china that Billingsley and Walker could make, John Rose was worried by the loss of custom with which he was threatened. There seems no doubt that John Rose's purchase of the Swansea works was due primarily to his anxiety to secure the services of Billingsley for himself. In the end, after his purchase of the Swansea works, he bought the plant, moulds, and everything else at Nantgarw, and made an agreement with Billingsley and Walker to make the same quality of china at Coalport for a period of seven years. Rose discovered that the process, however fine in its resultant body and texture, was an extremely costly one because the clay

The inscription on the back of the bicentenary plate

wanting in plasticity was difficult to work, and its soft body made it liable to melt or lose its shape if there was the least too much heat in the biscuit kiln.

About this time James Ryan discovered a very pure felspar in one of the Bredon hills which was considered nearer to the exact equivalent of the Chinese kaolin than Cornish clay and capable of imparting the egg-shell quality so much admired. So the *pâte dure* was substituted for the *pâte tendre* and by adding pure felspar to the Cornish stone and clay, which already contained a high percentage of it, a good translucent body was obtained more cheaply than by using a fret body.

About this time the Society of Arts offered a prize " to the person who shall discover the cheapest, safest, most durable and most easily fusible composition fit for the purposes of glazing earthenware without any preparation of lead, arsenic or other pernicious ingredients, and superior to any hitherto in use." The effect of the lead on the dippers was too often paralysis, and by now humane considerations were beginning to stir faintly, still very faintly, the surface of industry.

The gold Isis medal was awarded to John Rose, whose winning composition was—felspar from Welshpool, 27 parts ; borax, 18 parts ; sand from Lynn, Norfolk, 4 parts ; Cornish china-clay, 3 parts ; nitre, 3 parts ; soda, 3 parts. When this mixture had been fritted 2 parts of calcined borax were added.

Rose was proud of his success over competitors like Copelands, Davenports and other prominent manufacturers, and on some Coalport pieces the success was recorded by a tablet two inches in diameter inscribed : *J. Rose and Co., Coalport Felt Spar* (sic) *Porcelain. The gold medal awarded May 30th, 1820.*

Randall does not consider that the felspar porcelain was ever as pure or as transparent as the original Nantgarw fret body ware, and points out that no new element was introduced by using felspar because the kaolin contained in Cornish stone and clay had been and was still being used at Plymouth, Derby, Worcester, Caughley and Coalport, and a judicious mixture of this with bone to add phosphate of lime made good china, the combination producing the mellowness and the whiteness which " approached in a degree the qualities of old and oriental china."

A word about china-stone and -clay.  Père d'Entrecolles,

" To-morrow "

*Originated 1938*

who lived at King-te-chin, the site of the great porcelain manufactories in the Celestial Empire, during the early part of the eighteenth century said that the chiefs ingredients of Chinese porcelain were *kao-lin* and *pe-tun-tse*. The former was the decomposed felspar (more correctly feldspar) of our Cornish clay, the latter probably a fusible ingredient of the paste resembling the china-stone of Cornwall, which is a disintegrated granite rock consisting of a mixture of quartz, partially decomposed felspar, and scales of a micaceous mineral called gilbertite.

From the time that the Portuguese doubled the Cape of Good Hope and started to trade in Chinese porcelain, it became a natural ambition in Europe to imitate it, but for two centuries the European potters failed to produce a body like that of the hard Oriental ware. And then Böttcher did it. Böttcher was an apothecary's assistant in Berlin credited with having discovered a way to make gold, and so much pestered in consequence that he took refuge in Saxony where, while he was in the laboratory of an alchemist at Dresden, some crucibles he had been preparing assumed the character of Chinese porcelain.

At first he worked with a brown clay found near Meissen and produced a red ware ; then one day he noticed that the hair-powder he was using was uncommonly heavy and on investigation discovered that this unwelcome substitute for the wheaten flour of true hair-powder was the substance for which he was searching. John Schnorr, an iron-master, when riding near Aue, had noticed that a soft white earth was sticky to his horse's feet which he decided would make a profitable substitute for wheaten flour. Under the name of Schnorr's White Earth it was sold in large quantities for this purpose.

Augustus II, Elector of Saxony and King of Poland, was so much impressed by the importance of Böttcher's experiments, that when in 1709 he produced white porcelain Augustus kept him shut up with every comfort at Meissen to prevent his escaping with the secret. The greatest secrecy was maintained over Böttcher's method of manufacture ; the kaolin was brought in sealed bags by sworn persons, and its exportation was forbidden. The factory at Meissen was still in existence at the beginning of the Second World War and even then it was more like a fortress than a factory. The original workmen were closely confined and closely watched, and every workshop was inscribed *Be Secret Unto Death*. Nevertheless, in spite of all precautions, in 1718, a year before Böttcher's death, Stolzel, the chief workman at Meissen, escaped to Vienna. Gradually the manufacture of hard porcelain spread thence over Europe.

The Sèvres works established at St. Cloud had been making a ware with a coarse yellow paste since 1695. Then Réaumur imported kaolin and petuntse from China, and from 1727 to 1729 he was searching France to discover the equivalent nearer home. He was unsuccessful, and it was not until 1768 that kaolin was discovered near Limoges, thus allowing Sèvres to start the manufacture of hard porcelain in 1769.

To William Cookworthy, a Plymouth Quaker, is due the discovery of the china-clay and china-stone in Cornwall which made English porcelain a rival of Sèvres and Dresden. Cookworthy, who was born in 1705, was in business as a wholesale druggist in Plymouth, and in the course of his chemical studies he was impressed by the statement of Père d'Entrecolles alluded to above. Cook-

worthy may have visited Paris where the Jesuit father had
sent specimens of the Chinese kaolin and petuntse at the
time Réaumur was searching for equally suitable material
in France.

As early as 1745 Cookworthy was writing to a friend in
Cornwall to say that a " person from Virginia " had
discovered kaolin and petuntse there and had shown him
some specimens of porcelain alleged to have been made
from them. Cookworthy had his doubts about the honesty
of the ' person from Virginia.'

The exact date when William Cookworthy discovered
the genuine article in Cornwall is uncertain. It may have
been as early as 1750 that he discovered china-stone
at Tregonning Hill near Breage, and close by abundance
of kaolin. Later he discovered " immense quantities " of
both in the parish of St. Stephen's nearer to Plymouth, on
land belonging to Lord Camelford, who joined Cookworthy in establishing works at Plymouth for the
manufacture of hard paste.

*Chaffers* is disinclined to accept so early a date as 1750
for Cookworthy's discovery, chiefly because in a letter of
1760 Cookworthy says he has just returned from Cornwall
where he has been for his health, and gives an account of
of a method of distilling sea-water without mentioning
china-clay or china-stone. The omission to mention his
discovery in a letter is hardly strong enough grounds to
presume he had not made it. However, it was not until
March 1768 that Camelford and Cookworthy took out a
patent for " a kind of porcelain newly invented, composed
of moorstone, or growan and growan clay." Cookworthy
had become a proper Cornishman.

On February 22nd, 1770, an advertisement in Berrow's

*Worcester Journal* said : " China painters wanted. For the Plymouth new invented patent porcelain manufactory. A number of sober, ingenious artists, capable of painting in enamel or blue, may hear of constant employ by sending their prosposals to Thomas Frank in Castle Street, Bristol."

Soon after this the Plymouth works were transferred to Bristol, when Richard Champion bought all Cookworthy's interest in the Plymouth patent. Cookworthy himself retired from the world of porcelain and devoted the remaining years of his life until he died in 1780 to the Society of Friends. William Cookworthy is almost as great a name in the history of the advancement of English porcelain as Thomas Frye of Bow . . . but it is time to return to John Rose who, after his triumph in 1820, devoted his unbounded energy and his fine brain to building up the Coalport works into not merely the largest porcelain in England but possibly in the world. Business flourished steadily. Warehouses were opened in London, Manchester, Sheffield and Shrewsbury, and a large trade was done with dealers all over the country. Employment was steady, and on the whole relations between master and man were good.

Randall gives a picture of conditions not long before he himself joined the staff at Coalport.

There were at Coalport, as at other works of the kind elsewhere, an intelligent class of men, among potters and painters, as well as in other departments. . . . Painters especially had good opportunities for mental culture and obtaining information. Numbers worked together in a room, one sometimes reading for the benefit of the others, daily papers were taken, discussions were often raised, and in politics the sharp features of party were as defined as in the House of Commons itself. The rooms were nicely warmed, and a woman appointed to sweep up, to bring coals, to keep the tables clean, to wash up dishes, peel potatoes, and fetch water for those who, not living near, brought their meals with them. It is not surprising, therefore, that men, having such advantages, should sometimes rise to higher situations. Some became linguists, some schoolmasters, engineers, and contractors ; one, breakfasting with a bishop, whose daughter he afterwards married, saw upon the table some time since, a service painted by himself when a workman at Coalport. Some were singular characters : old Jocky Hill kept his hunter ; John Crowther, a very amiable fellow, exceedingly good natured, and always ready to do a favour to any one who asked him, lived quite a recluse, studying algebra and mechanics. He has suggested many improvements in locomotives, steam paddles, brakes, etc., etc., and had the honour of submitting to the Government the plan of terminating annuities, by which money at that time was raised to carry on the war, and by which we have been saved the burden—so far—of a permanent debt ; also of making other suggestions, which have been likewise adopted. He also invented a most ingenious almanack applicable to all time.

Coalport men were usually great politicians ; Hunt, Hetherington, Richard Carlile, Sir Francis Burdett, and Cobbett, had their disciples and admirers ; and such was the eagerness to get the Register, with its familiar gridiron on the cover, that a man had been despatched to Birmingham for it from one of the rooms, his shopmates undertaking to do his work for him whilst he was away.

The works themselves are ill designed and badly constructed, the greater portion of them having been put up at the latter end of the past and beginning of the present centuries, whilst other portions were added from time to time, with no regard to ventilation or other requirements of health. Consequently there are the most curious ins and outs, dropsical-looking roofs, bulging walls, and drooping floors, which have to be propped underneath, to support half a century's accumulations of china, accumulations amounting to hundreds and hundreds of tons in weight. In entering some of these unhealthy ateliers and passages strangers have to look well to their craniums. Some work-rooms have very stifling atmospheres, charged with clay or flint ; the biscuit-room notably so.

It will be remembered that work in such conditions was at least a twelve-hour day, for women and children as well as men. Yet it may be doubted if John Rose in his humbler moments ever wondered if those in his employment had the slightest cause to question his paternal interest in their well-being.

It has not been possible to find out if any refusal of paternal demands caused the strike at Coalport, which occurred in November 1833, and which Randal calls " a memorable event in the history of the works, so much so that in speaking of occurrences it is usual to the present time (forty years later) to ask in case of doubt if it happened before or subsequent to the strike."

However, certainly a main cause of the disagreement between John Rose and his workmen was over their right to a trade union. They had a sick society called their ' Pitcher" and they had a " Travelling Society" for helping those in search of employment, with branches in all centres of the trade. However, they wanted to belong to a trade union, one of those dangerous " Secret Societies" being formed to threaten the commercial security of the country. The repeal of the Combination Laws in 1824 had caused such alarm and despondency among the industrialists of Scotland that an enlightened measure had been hastily

" ANNIVERSARY "

*Originated during the Second World War*

amended the following year to protect the imagined threat to business. Still, it was no longer possible for a magistrate to send a man to gaol merely for belonging to a trade union, or no doubt the Shropshire magistrates would have sent half of John Rose's workmen to gaol.

It is worth while studying the indictment (reproduced on the following page) of the trades union by the Coalport employees who supported John Rose and helped him to carry on the works to a limited extent while the strike continued.

John Rose was evidently regarded by his neighbours as their defender against revolution, and to show their appreciation of his fight for a master's right to handle his men as he thought fit they subscribed to present him with a massive silver goblet. The stem of a vine was entwined round the base to form the handles and grow loaded with grapes round the rim of the cover.

On one side the goblet was thus inscribed :

## PRESENTED TO JOHN ROSE ESQ.,

OF

COALPORT CHINA MANUFACTORY

BY HIS

FRIENDS AND NEIGHBOURS

MARCH 3RD

1834

# AN ADDRESS
# TO THE PUBLIC,
## MORE PARTICULARLY TO THOSE INTERESTED IN THE
# Porcelain Trade.

WE, the undersigned, in behalf of the Operatives still in the employ of the COAL-PORT PORCELAIN MANUFACTORY, in consequence of the numerous Reports and libellous Documents issued by the Members of the Trades Union, think it our duty both towards ourselves, and also our Employers, to give to the Public A TRUE AND CORRECT STATEMENT of the manner in which this Manufactory is at present proceeding; and at the same time the reasons for our remaining in employment, contrary to the opinion of our Fellow-Workmen. We are confident that every thinking and well regulated mind, must, on the perusal of the following, be convinced that we have done our duty to our Employers, ourselves, and the Country at large. We take leave to disclaim all ill feeling towards those, who hold an opposite opinion; and we assert, that the present paper is not meant to reflect on them, but merely to repel those FALSE ASSERTIONS, in which some of them, have thought proper to indulge.

## *We vindicate our Proceedings on the following grounds:*

FIRSTLY,—THAT UNIONS AMONGST THE OPERATIVES CAN NEVER TEND PERMANENTLY TO RAISE THE PRICE OF ANY MANUFACTURED ARTICLE.
SECONDLY,—THAT IT IS IMPOSSIBLE TO FORM ANY SOCIETY OF THIS DESCRIPTION, THAT CAN BE LASTING AND EFFICIENT.
THIRDLY,—THAT THIS PARTICULAR ESTABLISHMENT WAS THE LAST, ON WHICH SUCH AN EXPERIMENT OUGHT TO HAVE BEEN TRIED.

In the first place then,—That Unions amongst the Operatives, can never tend permanently to raise prices, is answered by a self-evident proposition, amounting almost to an Axiom: viz.: That the price of Goods depends on the relative bearing of supply and demand; for as a rise in Prices is produced by a deficiency of the supply, as compared with the demand,—so low prices are occasioned by the supply being greater than the consumption. But what would be the consequence if the Prices were raised? *It is evident there would not be so much consumed; and consequently, a large number of Workmen thrown out of employ.* This would be the case in any species of Manufactured Goods, even of what may be termed Necessaries;—how much greater therefore would be the falling off in the consumption of *fancy goods,* the purchase of which, depends entirely on the taste and caprice of the Public.

This resolves itself into one simple truth, that " No Operations of the Unions can increase consumption;" and that the principal cause of low wages, arises from the excessive number of Workmen in every branch of industry.

Secondly,—That it is impossible to form any Society of this description, that can be lasting and efficient, is equally clear; as is well observed in a very able Pamphlet on this subject, that, "The Elements of a Permanent Union do not exist among Operatives;" differing too much in sentiment, and too jealous of one another, ever to agree long together. Besides, men depending on the daily labour of their hands, are not in a condition to dictate to their employers; their wants being too immediate to allow them to refuse, for any length of time, employment even at a moderate remuneration. The Union with all its "Gigantic power," will never be able to prevent this; and, "The laws of nature will be found more imperative, than the laws of the Union."

In the third case,—That this particular Establishment was the last, on which such an experiment ought to have been made, *was the expressed opinion of those who now arrange themselves as its most bitter enemies:* neither can they deny, that they have experienced more liberty and liberality—more constant employment—and, less oppression—than ever they found under any other masters. And if there is any ground of complaint, it must be laid to the extreme generosity of Mr. ROSE, in striving to find, in bad times, employment for a *surplus number of hands,* to the detriment of his own pocket, and to the injury of old workmen.

WE hope the above will satisfy the Country, that we are not acting from selfish views, but from sound and true principles, in refusing to join a secret Society, whose whole object would not be revealed, till an illegal Oath was administered, which was meant to bind us to resolutions, we have too good reason for thinking, would be prejudicial to the best interests of the Country. And those few amongst us, who have been persuaded by their associates to enrol themselves Members, but who have also made a timely retreat from a Society, which they felt in cooler moments, was embracing objects incompatible with the good of the Trade, do not hesitate in declaring they feel *perfectly justified* within themselves, for having acted as they have; justly considering they committed an error, in being hurried away by the general feeling around them; but that it would be a two-fold error in adhering to a System, which in their consciences, they could not approve. We beg leave at the same time, to assure the Public, that notwithstanding what is said to the contrary, this Manufactory is proceeding in a satisfactory and successful manner, employing at this present time, about FOUR HUNDRED Persons, who are willing to serve to their utmost their present Masters, not as his '*Slaves,*' but as Men, who have the right to dispose of their labour at the best price they can fairly obtain, without wishing to dictate or interfere with the internal management of the concern, which always found us employment through the most depressed period. We still rely on our Employers only for justice—and they on us for exertion.

| | | | |
|---|---|---|---|
| John Hughes | B. T. Goodwin | John Jones | Thomas Bagshaw |
| Hamlet Stevens | James Rouse | William Worrall | John Greatbatch |
| Thomas Dixon | Thomas Speak | Peter Stephan | George Mansell |
| Edward Jones | John Culliss | William Stephan | John Poole |
| Abraham Milner | Josiah Patten | Henry Stephan | William Aston |
| Thomas Hayward | J. H. Smith | George Aston | John Leighton |
| Joseph Birbeck | W. Street | Joseph Harper | Enoch Nevitt |

*Printed by W. SMITH, Post-Office, Ironbridge.*

*Indictment connected with the Trade Union dispute. Extracts from this document are printed on page 125*

On the other side the goblet was inscribed :

TRIBUTE OF RESPECT

TO HIS

PUBLIC AND PRIVATE CHARACTER

AND TO THE

UNCOMPROMISING FIRMNESS

WITH WHICH

HE HAS RECENTLY RESISTED THE

DEMANDS OF AN ILLEGAL

CONSPIRACY

It was no doubt a source of much gratification to the neighbours that the illegal conspirators had suffered acute hardship and privation during those winter months.

In spite of this industrial upheaval Coalport continued to prosper. Thousands of pounds were spent on experiments in an attempt to reproduce the famous Turquoise of Sèvres, but all that was achieved for some years was a pale imitation called Celeste. Later a much better colour was produced by Thomas Bagshaw, whose name is among the signatories of the anti-trade union manifesto as also are the names of three Stephans. Stephan may be recalled as one of the artists Thomas Turner brought back with him to Caughley : these are his sons.

The imitations at Coalport of Sèvres were so faithful that to this day they deceive experts. Nor did the artists of Coalport confine themselves to the patterns and colour of Sèvres ; they counterfeited also the marks, not only the double L's of Royal Sèvres which were forbidden after Louis XVI was executed but also the crossed swords of Dresden and Chelsea's golden anchor. Experts had to remind collectors of old green Chelsea that the anchor might come from Severn and not from Thames, that the raised flowers and the "Berlin chain edge" of Dresden might never have been east of Harwich.

Of the egg-shell china produced at Coalport during the reign of John Rose Llewellynn Jewitt observes :

> The examples I have examined appear to be much finer than any others which have come under my notice, for the fact that the body is *pure porcelain*, being composed of one stone and one clay alone, unmixed with bone or any other material whatever.

When John Rose died in 1841 the Coalport china works passed to Charles Maddison, William Pugh, Thomas Rose, and William Frederick Rose. Thomas Rose was the brother who had started an opposition business when John Rose moved to Coalport from Jackfield. William Frederick Rose was his son.

John Rose was buried at Barrow where just over thirty years before Thomas Turner was laid to rest in the same churchyard. The inscription on his tomb reads, " He was the founder of the China Manufactory at Coalport and died beloved and respected of all who knew him." Rose expanded Coalport to a size that Turner never dreamed of for Caughley, but the foundation of its prosperity was the Willow Pattern, and the old blue china of Caughley. One can speculate whether John Rose behaved as well as he might have behaved to Thomas Turner. No matter, they lie within a few yards of one another in the old churchyard, for ever at peace now. And the snowdrops that pattern the ground between their graves during each February that goes by seem like sprays and sprigs from the old china which both men gave so much of themselves to beautify.

In 1843 the proprietors of the Coalport china works, still known as " Messrs. John Rose and Company ", were William Pugh, who had joined the firm as a partner in 1839, and William Frederick Rose who was able to carry on the business as successfully as his redoubtable uncle and even to develop it on the artistic side.

In 1845 Messrs. Daniell, the big china dealers, were commanded by Queen Victoria to prepare a dessert service as a present to the Czar Nicholas I, the manufacture of which was entrusted to Coalport. It was a typically early Victorian piece of solid richness, being coloured in Royal blue and decorated round the rim in six separate bands with the various orders of the Russian Empire and the eagles of Russia and Poland in the centre. This was exhibited at the Great Exhibition in 1851 and caused a sensation. So too, did a dessert service in rose du Barry, the equal of the famous rose Pompadour of Sèvres, the art of making which had been lost in the turmoil of the Revolution. In 1849 Daniell had suggested the attempts being made and in the following year George Hancock, the colour-maker at Coalport, after repeated experiments was successful. This dessert service caused an even greater sensation than the Queen's present to the Czar, when it was exhibited in 1851.

In awarding a Prize Medal the Jurors put on record :

Rose J., and Co., Coalbrook Dale, Shropshire, have exhibited porcelain services and other articles, which have attracted special attention of the Jury. A dessert service of a rose ground is in particular remarkable, not only as being the nearest approach we have seen to the famous colour which it is designed to imitate, but for the excellence of the flower-painting, gilding, and other decorations, and the hardness and transparency of the glaze. The same observation applied to other porcelain articles exhibited by this firm. The Jury have awarded to Messrs. Rose and Co. a Prize Medal.

There was a fine appropriateness in the firm of John Rose and Company's achieving their supreme triumph with this revived rose. Lord Ashburton was the lucky purchaser of this beautiful dessert set. Other sets in rose du Barry were made for the Emperor of the French, and many English noblemen and French connoisseurs. The success of Coalport at the Great Exhibition was repeated at the first World's Fair in Chicago in the 'fifties. Every piece was sold and there were many orders : the appreciation the American public showed then of Coalport ware has lasted a century and is to-day keener than ever.

In 1855 at the Great French Exhibition, Coalport china received a medal. About that time William Frederick Rose went to Paris in the company of Daniell, the dealer, who visited Sèvres and was taken round the works. Rose, feeling that it might be considered a breach of etiquette, would not accompany Daniell on his tour, and remained outside. When the Sèvres manager heard who Daniell's friend was, he insisted on showing him round as well. Then with *empressement* he told Rose that he was at liberty to send his best artists to copy anything at Sèvres that pleased their fancy, and sometime after this many of the Sèvres moulds were sent over to Coalport. It is a pleasant story on the surface, but it is difficult not to feel that William Rose ought to have replied *timeo Danaos et dona ferentes*, for undoubtedly this copying of other ware was not to the ultimate benefit of Coalport.

"NUMBER 2665"

*Known at the Works as "Panel"*
*Originated 1896*

"ADORATION"

*Originated 1949*

In 1862 came the London Exhibition which brought another medal, but something was wrong. Incidentally, the Exhibition itself was not a success. The death of the Prince Consort had taken the spirit out of the enterprise. The Queen remained in the seclusion of her own grief, and it had to be opened on her behalf by the Duke of Cambridge. The Royal cortège arrived at the opening like a funeral with the servants all in black livery and the many distinguished guests in " trappings and suits of woe."

# III

## *Coalport Under the Bruffs*

LATER ON in the year 1862 William Frederick Rose retired from business, and William Pugh became the sole proprietor of the works. He seems to have been a muddler ; when he died in June 1875 the whole business was in confusion. William Pugh's brother, Charles, who had married Martha Rose, a daughter of Thomas Rose, and Charles Pugh's brother-in-law, Edmund Ratcliff, were left executors ; to adjust the claims of them and of many others the estate was put into chancery, one Gelson being appointed as receiver and manager.

The stock was immense ; it had been accumulating for fifty years, and it was now suddenly thrown on the market. Hundreds of dozens of the well-loved pattern called the Indian Tree which had remained out of sight for forty years were brought to light. A hundred dozen or so of printed saucers would be found stowed away without cups to match ; scores of piles of white plates and dishes, sixteen or eighteen feet high, which had been sorted and set aside for some fault, were discovered. " It speaks well for the quality of the china," says Randall, " that the biscuit and glaze are both sound and good."

Here and there in the warehouses the floors were giving way under the huge weight of stock they were having to carry. In one room a large amount of old Caughley china was discovered, untouched since John Rose had brought it down across the river on the heads of women sixty years earlier from warehouses on the site of which cattle now grazed. In another room a number of Caughley copper-plates was found; these had been engraved by Herbert Minton's father.

Randall suggests that this unwieldy stock had been allowed to accumulate as a result of the determination of John Rose and his nephew to keep their workmen employed. It seems fairly clear, however, that William Pugh had been quite unable to handle the business after the retirement of William Rose.

A good example of his lack of grip appeared in the course of an action for the recovery of the price fixed for a Sèvres service, part of which turned out to be a Coalport imitation of Old Sèvres.

During the adjournment Mr. Cock, Q.C., counsel for the defence, told his learned opponent, Mr. Kempe, Q.C., and Mr. Frederic Litchfield, the Editor of *Chaffers*, who was being called as an expert witness, an anecdote about William Pugh. Pugh, anxious to improve his productions, bought in London for about £600 what he believed was a particularly fine specimen of old Sèvres. Having secured this vase of good form and beautiful colour, he took it with him to his works at Coalport and showed it to his head-foreman as an object lesson in excellence of craftsmanship. He then instructed him to make every effort to bring the Coalport products up to such a standard. The foreman replied that this ought not to be too difficult because the vase in question had been made at Coalport some years previously.

When the Court assembled, Mr. Cock in his speech for the defence began to use this anecdote as an argument for the jury to show how close some imitations could be. However, his learned friend, Mr. Kempe, at once objected on the grounds that as Mr. Pugh was not to be called as a witness the anecdote was inadmissible, and the judge decided in favour of Mr. Kempe.

This sidelight upon William Pugh and Coalport during the years after William Rose left the firm is doubly illuminating. It reveals that Pugh himself was not a master of his job and at the same time how much workmanship was being expended on imitation. Once an artist, a newspaper, or a manufactory takes that road the end sooner or later will always prove to be a dead one.

Information is wanting about the decade that followed the death of William Pugh, which very lack of information suggests that the prestige of Coalport was steadily declining, not to mention its commercial position. Family quarrels did not help a recovery of the situation.

About 1885 the Coalport works was bought by Peter Schuyler Bruff, an eminent engineer, residing at Ipswich. No record exists of why an eminent East Anglian engineer should suddenly have risked his capital in an industry of which he cannot have had any practical experience and of which the stability must by now have begun to seem uncertain. It may be that he was advised by experts that he was being offered a bargain if he could get the best technical assistance to enable him to take advantage of the bargain.

We know nothing of the first four years of Coalport under Peter Schuyler Bruff, but in 1889 Charles Bruff, his son, came back on leave from India where he was engaged on Government work as an engineer, and during this vacation he paid a visit to his father's china-works that was to have a profound influence on the future of Coalport.

Charles Bruff had imagination and ready sympathy with a great deal of nervous energy and the precious gift of being able to concentrate passionately on the object which had stirred his imagination. He looked round the works in that wooded Shropshire valley, decided that opportunities of developing the place on the right lines were being lost ; in short he fell in love with the notion of restoring Coalport to the high place it had once occupied. No doubt he recognised that the advantages, conferred once upon a time by the proximity of coal and various kinds of clay to such a waterway as the Severn and the now abandoned canal no longer existed, and therefore that Coalport had to be thoroughly reorganised to adapt itself to the change in conditions all over the country. It was as an enlightened man of business that Charles Bruff viewed the potentialities of Coalport and of Coalport china. His enthusiasm having been roused, Charles Bruff wasted no time in giving it practical expression. He threw up his job in India and told his father that he was ready to tackle Coalport. Peter Schuyler Bruff immediately turned the firm into a private limited liability company under the title of the Coalport China Company (John Rose and Co.) with himself as founder and governing director, and his son Charles G. Bruff as managing director.

Charles Bruff lost no time in imparting his own vitality to the languishing business, and with brilliant adaptability set to work to make a good potter of an engineer. He gathered round him talented artists, skilled craftsmen, and good commercial brains. He announced that the future policy of Coalport would be to revive old designs with all the beauty and grace of once upon a time ; to introduce new designs and patterns ; to encourage originality and avoid imitations. This policy was resolutely put into effect.

The *British Museum Guide* would not be able to say of Coalport china with the new mark of the crown with England above and Coalport below :

" Marks of other factories, such as Sèvres and Chelsea, were not uncommonly used on careful copies of these factories made at Coalport."

Not again would an expert like Professor A. H. Church be able to observe severely :

" The vases are often coarse imitations of Chelsea porcelain, and sometimes bear what must be looked upon as the forged mark of an anchor in gold. Cups and saucers are also found having two L's crossed in imitation of Sèrves ; marks of other factories, English and foreign, are also found upon pieces of Coalport porcelain and earthenware."

Within a few years Charles Bruff had pulled the historic china works together. At the Chicago World's Fair of 1893 Coalport ware enjoyed a signal success and thereafter the American and Canadian markets were thoroughly exploited. The works were extended and in part rebuilt. Employment was given to over five hundred workpeople in the lively hope that industry could after all be main-

"Number 9309"
*Originated 1935*

"Golden Wedding"
*Originated 1939*

tained in a rural district in spite of having lost the peculiar advantages of its situation. The Shropshire coalfield might no longer depend on its little port ; the Severn might no longer be a great commercial waterway ; the cargoes of china-clay and china-stone might no longer be rounding Land's End and beating their way up the Bristol Channel ; the Coalbrookdale Iron Works, which in 1766 had for the first time produced wrought-iron from pig-iron without using a blast, might no longer seem one of the chief centres of a great industry. Nevertheless, as Blacker says in *Nineteenth-Century Ceramic Art*, quoting from a Staffordshire newspaper :

> A unanimity of pride in Coalport ware and its Shropshire home pervades the establishment ; and is the natural outcome of Mr. Bruff's own forceful inspiration. He has just undertaken the managing directorship of Messrs. Craven, Dunhill and Co., Ltd., a well-known firm of encaustic tiles and ceramic mosaic manufacturers, having works on the farther side of the river [i.e. at Jackfield]. A busy man in every sense, Mr. Bruff has made Coalport the centre of an interest which pulses with the love of Art in some of its daintiest forms.

In 1898 the board of directors was joined by Charles Bruff's brother-in-law, A. N. Garrett, and in 1900 Peter Schuyler Bruff died.

An indication of Coalport's recovery may be perceived in the visit to the works that year by Queen Mary, then Duchess of York. She was presented with a tea service and a shape of tea ware was named York Shape in her honour.

Yet although during the first years of the present century the Coalport China Company was pulled round financially, although the Bruff régime had given new life not only to the Coalport works but also to the whole locality and although the reputation of the firm's products had been completely restored, the profits were never large, and with the advent of the First World War and the trading slump and labour troubles that followed, the company was involved in moderate but disagreeably steady losses. A strike of thirteen weeks by the employees in 1923 caused by a five per cent reduction in wages was a bad financial set-back and much upset Charles Bruff personally, for he had been genuinely devoted to the well-being of his work-people without any of that early Victorian capacity to wear blinkers of sentiment about such devotion while it plodded on steadily in the direction of the main chance. One may suspect John Rose of an ability to suppose that the provision of coffins for his drowned workpeople at his own expense compensated for failing to provide them with proper surroundings in which to work a twelve- or fourteen-hour day. Charles Bruff seems to have been a genuinely enlightened employer.

In 1923 the works showed a loss of about £3,700. In 1924 they showed a loss of nearly £2,500. In that year the Bruff family and their associates sold the business to Cauldon Potteries Limited, and in 1926 the Coalport works was moved to Shelton in Staffordshire. A fairly large number of the Coalport people continued to work for the company, some coming over daily by omnibus, others settling down in the Potteries.

A sprinkling of those remain in the Crescent works in Stoke-upon-Trent where Coalport china is made to-day, and one of these, Mr. Leonard Barber, a caster, has given us some reminiscences of the Bruff régime, going back

"HAZELTON"
*Originated 1939*

"MASTERPIECE"
*Originated 1949*

sixty years, which testify to Charles Bruff's honest benevolence.

When the young Len Barber was apprenticed at Coalport, he was put in a workshop with several journeymen who often used to talk of Charles Bruff's first arrival at Coalport in 1889. He introduced himself to his future employees by holding a smoking-concert in one of the workshops at which many speeches were made. It was " a very jovial evening " and after it that particular workshop was always known as " The Happy Home " which had been the keynote of the evening's eloquence.

Mr. Barber recalls that the river flowed immediately under the windows of the first workshop in which he worked and how once he was able to tell the works bricklayer, who was a member of the Ironbridge Angling Society, that a trout had been rising just outside the shop door. The angler spent most of his dinner hour fishing for that trout, and just as the bell tolled for the afternoon spell of work the inmates of the shop had the pleasure of seeing the works bricklayer hook and land a two-and-a-half-pounder. Mr. Barber recalls further how often in his next shop he had seen the Wheatland Hunt pass through the Hay Farm fields on one side of the Works. " The hounds on occasion being in full cry and a very pleasing sight we used to think it."

Well, of course, we are all inclined to fancy that things were better and jollier and brighter when we were young, for when we were young enjoyment was fresh ; but nobody will blame Mr. Barber for reflecting a little wistfully that whatever other advantages Stoke may enjoy hounds are not seen in full cry outside the Crescent works and the rings of a rising trout do not write themselves in silver upon that particular reach of the Trent.

Mr. Barber in recalling the savage winter of 1894-95, when the ice on the Severn was a foot thick and was sometimes piled up to twenty feet in blocks before the March thaw, recalls that Charles Bruff ran a soup kitchen for the villagers' children at his own house throughout that winter.

In 1897 Bruff gave a tea-party with sports for all the children of Coalport when each child was presented with a china mug inscribed *Queen Victoria's Diamond Jubilee.* The small children were given quarter-pints, the bigger ones half-pints. " That is the only record my family ever held," Mr. Barber adds. " We had the most mugs."

Two or three years after this Mr. and Mrs. Bruff were visited by two maiden ladies from Scotland at a time when the youth of Coalport was getting " rather a poor name. We used to play pranks such as changing neighbours' gates and numerous other little items." These two ladies took the part of youth and persuaded Mr. Bruff to open a recreation room. " And did we appreciate those ladies ? We would have done anything for them. I think most of us worshipped them in our way."

In our days when welfare is taken for granted Mr. Barber's memory of the lectures they used to have on beekeeping or gardening or what not may seem trivial enough to some ; others will find a fragrance in such a memory, for those two maiden ladies from Scotland are imprinted on the mind of a craftsman as fadeless and dainty as the patterns on the china he has cast. Another pleasant memory is the delight of Charles Bruff " if he could only catch any of his workpeople walking in the vicinity of his house. What pleasure it gave him to invite them inside his grounds and show them round his flower-beds and instruct his gardener to pluck them a handful of flowers each, especially when the daffodils were about."

The youth of the village had the run of Mr. Bruff's fields for football and cricket. Mr. Barber cannot remember anyone's asking his permission. "They just took it for granted." Those words say much.

By June, 1902, Bruff had practically rebuilt the works, and in the last group of buildings he placed a slab which was inscribed *June 1902 Coronation*. From those early days Mr. Barber recalls that the company used to hold sales of china in the Coalport coffee house which was then used for the works messroom and canteen. These sales drew buyers from all over the district, and the packers were kept busy packing the customers' purchases. The women decorators and warehouse people were in attendance at the stalls, and the opening of one of those sales was like a small exhibition. The children welcomed the occasion, because they could always earn a few coppers by carrying hampers and parcels to the railway station and elsewhere. Mr. Barber remembers well the visit of the Duchess of York and the cheering crowds in the village. Old people told him that such crowds had not been seen in Coalport since their parents turned out to see the launching of the first iron boat ever built at Coalport wharf, the foundations of which may still be traced in the boundary of what used to be the Coalport china works. The boat was built at the Willey foundry near Broseley, and the attraction to the neighbours was their firm belief that a boat built of iron would immediately sink to the bottom of the river. When it floated they were inclined to suspect black magic.

It was from the old Coalport wharf that Captain Matthew Webb learned to swim, walking over from Dawley to take his daily dip. When Dawley erected a monument to the memory of the Channel swimmer the Coalport China Company turned out memorial mugs with a portrait of Matthew Webb.

Mr. Barber is apologetic for remembering more about

*Design on mug in memory of Capt. Matthew Webb, the first man to swim the Channel. It was from the old Coalport wharf that Webb learnt to swim*

Mr. Bruff's human side than his contributions to the art of fine bone china. He remembers in the railway strike of 1911 gathering wood for fuel with some of his friends near Mr. Bruff's house and Mr. Bruff's coming out and telling them they could fell any of the trees growing on his side of the road. He remembers Mr. Bruff's helping the stationmaster to make a station garden to compete for the prize offered by the London and North Western Railway and how thanks to him the little station won the first prize three years in succession. He remembers Dr. Fox Edwards' attributing a case of typhoid to the foul condition of the old canal which ran through the village and how Mr. Bruff persuaded the owners, the old London and North Western Railway, to have it filled in, to the great relief of the village.

His chief memory of Mr. Bruff's ideas for china is of a tea-pot with a short spout and a kind of lock lid and of a coffee-pot with a lock lid. He can still make them as he learned to make them long ago. He was too young to understand what it meant for Coalport china to be awarded the gold medal at the Chicago Exhibition of 1893 for its body of fine bone china ; but he remembers Mr. John Davidson, a big dealer from America who used to come every year to stay with Mr. Bruff, and how when he went back to the United States the workpeople used to say that Coalport was sure of being able to carry on for another twelve months. Then Mr. Davidson died, and the American dealer who followed him was not so keen on Coalport china. This may have contributed to the straitness of the finances.

Not long ago Mr. Barber went to the pageant in Hanley Park that commemorated the bicentenary of the birth of

Josiah Wedgwood. One of the scenes showed a strike and the strikers hurling brickbats. It set Mr. Barber off thinking about the Coalport strike in 1923, and recalling what an orderly affair it was in comparison. He remembers Mr. Bruff announcing that the firm had lost £6,000 during the previous year and that it would be necessary to make a cut in wages. The workpeople thought that the losses could be saved in other directions. " Zero hour was fixed for the Friday evening. Here my memory fails, for I don't remember if Mr. Bruff wanted to meet a deputation of the workpeople and they would not meet him without the union official or whether they did meet him. However, nothing came of it and the workers did not resume work the following day. Mr. Bruff refused to meet the union official and both parties were very stubborn. Work was not resumed for thirteen weeks. Then we went back to work on terms that could have been settled in the first place ; we accepted a drop in wages but not as much as we were asked to accept at first. It was an unofficial strike in the beginning, but it was recognised by the union when all the facts were put before it."

There is no doubt that this strike was a severe blow to Charles Bruff. It wounded his affections, and it will be admitted that the picture of the man which emerges from Mr. Barber's memory of him does reveal a true love of his workpeople quite untainted by early Victorian self-deception. It was a profound shock to Coalport when he sold the business and the works were removed to the Potteries. The old Coalport works in the fabric of which are incorporated the bricks of the old Salopian China Warehouse of Caughley and Thomas Turner's *château*, Caughley Place, are to-day devoted to the production of

FLOWER GROUP

"BARBARA"

*Originated 1949*

FLOWER GROUP

rubber mats, etc., from old rubber. The smokeless kilns are cold ; the barges no longer tie up to the wharf on their way to Bristol, and never a wagon rumbles over the Iron Bridge; but the trout still rise in Severn below the trees of Swynney Cliff and Tarbach Dingle as they rose when Len Barber was a boy, and Len Barber himself is still casting his tea-pots in Stoke as he learnt to cast them in Coalport long ago. Time may be marching on, but his scythe sometimes drags behind him, and the sound is an agreeable one.

# IV

## Coalport Goes to Stoke

THE CAULDON POTTERIES which bought the Coalport China Company from Charles Bruff and his associates in 1925 was an old establishment in Cauldon Place, Shelton, founded by Job Ridgway, a former apprentice of Wedgwood's. He took his sons John and William into partnership, but died in 1814. From that date until 1830 John and William remained in partnership. Then they separated because John thought William too wildly speculative. William took over another works, and John stayed soberly at Cauldon Place until he retired in 1858. He made a dessert service decorated with the Royal Arms for Queen Victoria in 1855.

At the time the Coalport China Company was acquired by Cauldon Potteries the latter was controlled by Mr. H. T. Robinson and his associates, in 1932, and in a few years it went into liquidation. Then through a director of the firm the Coalport China Company bought Cauldon Potteries. Four years later the Coalport Group was acquired by George Jones and Sons, Ltd., and it was moved to the Crescent Works, Stoke-upon-Trent. The latter business since 1932 had been mostly owned by Harrison and Son

FLOWER GROUP      " ISOBEL "      " JENNIFER "      BIRDBATH

*Originated 1949*

(Hanley), Ltd., of whom more anon. In 1947 the Harrison company became disassociated from George Jones and Sons, Ltd., and Mr. S. T. Harrison and his son, Mr. Stanley Harrison, became sole proprietors of the Jones Group including the Coalport China Company.

George Jones who founded his firm in 1850 had served his apprenticeship with Minton's and soon built up a good reputation for himself as a maker of fine bone china.

S. T. Harrison and his son, Stanley Harrison, who now own George Jones and Sons, Ltd., Cauldon Potteries and the Coalport China Company are not potters, but their firm for years has produced many of the materials required in the manufacture of pottery—ceramic colours, stains and oxides, and many kinds of glazes ; they go back for the origins of their business to the year 1810.

A large slice of Hanley, including the present site of the Phoenix Chemical Works, the headquarters of Harrison and Sons, was once known as Hall Fields, and in 1728 this land was owned by Thomas Smith. In 1806 John Smith, the great-grandson of Thomas, sold a portion of his estate to George Fox of Burslem, a colour maker, and again in 1808 and 1809 two other plots. The land which George Fox bought was set back a little from Market Street with a frontage on a street that was not yet built, now Bath Street. By 1811 George Fox had erected buildings on the land he had acquired.

George Fox died in 1829, after which the land passed through the ownership of several colour makers until some time between 1850 and 1860 it came into the possession of Joseph Wooliscroft Goodwin, colour maker.

A few miles to the north-east of Stoke-upon-Trent, a short distance from the main road between Stone and

Leek lies the ancient village of Stanley whence came at the end of the twelfth century the first Stanley in the great line of the Earls of Derby.

At the foot of the steep hill on which the village stands there is a valley down which runs a stream, the head of which was dammed in 1840 to form Stanley Pool as a reservoir to feed the canals system. At the foot of the dam was a small mill used for grinding flint by water wheel. In the middle of the valley was another water cornmill known as the Stanley Mill. Four hundred yards farther down the stream was another water cornmill known as the Walk Mill which was later converted into a flint mill and as such in 1856 was acquired by Joseph Goodwin.

William Richard Harrison was a wholesale chemist in Banbury whence he used to supply all the chemists within range of a pony and trap. In 1868 he went to the potteries and bought for £800 the Bath Street property in the occupation of Goodwin from the Trustees of the Manchester and Liverpool District Banking Company. Later in the same year he bought from Goodwin the Walk Mill for £1,355. This was now described as a Stream and Water Colour Mill. In 1871 William Richard Harrison took his eldest son Thomas William into partnership with him on a fifteen years' agreement. William Richard Harrison never went to live in Staffordshire and the whole responsibility for the development of the business rested upon Thomas William Harrison who during the 'eighties and 'nineties of the last century had the help of two of his younger brothers—Charles and Neil. By 1884 the Stanley Water Cornmill had become two cottages with a flint mill adjoining ; this T. W. Harrison bought from the Alton Mill Company together with the top flint mill. In 1887 he

" MARILYN "

SUNDIAL

*Originated 1949*

" ROSALINDA "

had extended it and renamed it the Hercules Mill. In 1884 he had also acquired two water meadows and in the following year entered into an agreement with the North Staffordshire Railway Company to construct the siding from Endon Station to Victoria Mill, the new name given to the old Walk Mill. Four large mills now grind raw materials for the Ceramic Industry to the requisite fineness. These materials include flint, stone, felspar, whiting and quartz.

In 1870 T. W. Harrison built the Providence building in Wilson Street, Hanley, and in 1897 he pulled down a number of cottages in Wilson Street and in partnership with George P. Rataud and his son, S. T. Harrison, built on the site the Tintorex Works, forming themselves into the Potters Decorative Supply Company. The Tintorex Works was burnt down in 1904, and the land passed into the possession of Harrison and Son (Hanley), Ltd., in 1906.

In 1905 the Old Hall Porcelain Company, Ltd., which had works covering the whole of the Bath Street site, some of whose land had been bought by T. W. Harrison in 1900, passed out of existence. A portion of their land was owned by Gaspard Jakober, a colour manufacturer, and when he died his heirs sold the land to Harrison and Son. In 1919 the remaining ground down to Hill Street was purchased from the Old Hall Estate Company, Ltd. Finally more land was bought at Joiners Square between 1907 and 1929 : that consisted in part of the site of the Trent Pottery. Such in brief is the history of the site on which the Phoenix Chemical Works now stands.

T. W. Harrison had a tremendous struggle to build up what is now one of the largest firms of colour makers in the pottery industry. Every property and piece of land he bought was at once mortgaged, and sometimes remortgaged. The last major mortgage was paid off in 1908. T. W. Harrison retired to Bournemouth in 1906 and died on September 30th, 1909. His sons, Sydney Thomas Harrison and Arthur Cecil Harrison and his grandsons, Stanley Harrison, and Bernard Harrison, son of A. C. Harrison, carried on with equal vigour a great tradition of enterprise through four generations of a family. In 1936 Mr. Stanley Harrison took over the control of the Crescent Works on behalf of the firm of Harrison & Sons, Ltd., until, as previously mentioned, he and his father became the sole proprietors of the business in 1947.

We may seem to have wandered rather a long way from the making of fine bone china, and yet not so far when we remember the importance of colour in that art. It is meet that the Coalport China Company which owed so much to Thomas Turner's blue, and Samuel Walker's maroon and John Rose's rose du Barry should now be directed by a maker of colour.

"Breeze" Wishing Well "Judith Anne"

*Originated 1949*

# V

## *Coalport To-day*

IN SPITE of the complicated shifts since Charles Bruff sold Coalport to the Cauldon Potteries, rather painfully related in the preceding chapter, the Coalport China Company housed in the Crescent Works at Stoke-upon Trent still retains its own individuality, its own personality, its own identity in a word. It may share the works with two other companies, but its own unique traditions of production and craftsmanship are most sedulously and most jealously preserved in its own quarters.

The Crescent Works are extensive; they cover some five acres, and at the moment they are being modernised with the object of streamlining the complicated processes of pottery. It is so long since we were allowed to buy any coloured china in this country that we are apt to forget it is still being made. There is some consolation in knowing that hand-painted fine china from Coalport made at the Crescent Works was never in greater demand than it is to-day in the United States and Canada. As these words are written, overseas orders for Coalport china are so great that they have entailed a three-years' production programme. It is a coincidence of happy omen that the

Crescent was almost the earliest mark on the ware of the old Salopian China Warehouse at Caughley.

Perhaps the predominant impression to stamp itself on the mind in the course of the lengthy tour of the works that we undertook is the condition of continuous change in which a successful pottery produces its ware. Old processes are constantly giving way to newer methods ; new plant is being installed alongside earlier machinery ; new traditions in patterns and design are being built up, while at the same time old traditions of long standing and proven value are carefully preserved. And so, as we journeyed through the works we began to receive the curious sensation of looking back through two centuries of the production of fine china and of witnessing present and future progress in its manufacture.

During the last twelve months far reaching changes have been introduced into the works. Mr. Eardley, who is the director responsible for the general management of the firm, showed us some of these conversions and additions which have taken place to enable the output of fine china to meet the continuously increasing demands of customers in North America. The modern shops with improved methods of lighting, heating and ventilation, the latest types of plant and machinery have been designed to make the production of fine china a pleasant and interesting occupation under conditions vastly different from those experienced in the early days at Coalport.

Time and war have played their part in reducing the ranks of the artists and workers who migrated from Coalport to Stoke twenty-five years ago. During the recent war the firm lost many of their highly skilled employees, who were recruited into work of national

*Mr. Arthur Howell, China Biscuit Warehouseman. He joined the firm in 1904*

importance, and some of these have not returned. Nevertheless, the Coalport traditions are still more than adequately represented and ensured by several outstanding personalities. Foremost among them is the firm's art director, Mr. Percy Simpson, who presides over decoration. In the multifarious duties that such a responsibility entails one wonders how he finds time for his own designs on which he works in a minute studio that looks more like an office. He does find the time somehow, and the patrons of Coalport will testify how much he has contributed to their pleasure in fine ware.

Mr. Simpson took us through shop after shop in his decorating department, and we were able to watch scores of women and girls at work on the delicate enamelling and gilding processes, some of them being trained by the old mistresses in executing the fine work required of them, others already experts in their craft and producing results equally as good as their predecessors' at Coalport. And here, too, among the paintresses we found another representative of old Coalport in the person of Miss Violet Moreton, and that was another pleasant link with the past.

Nobody could pass from room to room in which women and girls were at work with their brushes without reflecting how far their bright occupation seemed from the notion so many have that industry to-day is almost always a monotonous and repetitive task in the performance of which the individual seems to become the slave of the machine he is controlling. The atmosphere resembled rather that of an *atelier* full of earnest students than the workshop of a factory.

At this point we should retrace our steps because decoration is, as anyone knows, the end of the long sequence

*Mr. Percy Simpson, Art Director, who joined the firm in 1901, with Mr. Stanley Harrison*

of processes which go to the making of finished china-ware. Between the slip-house where the three ingredients of fine bone china—the clay, the stone and the bone—are weighed out and mixed and the decorating department, the operations are so considerable and involved that they include over seventy separate occupations. Many of these occupations in the groundlaying, printing, burnishing and other processes call for the highest skill which can only come from years of training and experience. Here again the value of the sprinkling of the Coalport survivors comes into play. In the casting department, for instance, we found Mr. Leonard Barber, whose reminiscences of " Coalport under the Bruffs " have figured in the preceding chapter. In the biscuit-ware department we found another old Coalport man in Mr. Arthur Howell who, like Mr. Barber, spoke with affection of the old days on the banks of the Severn.

In the printing department we met yet another Coalport worthy who handles the printing press. This was Mr. Frederick Ellis and it was welcome to find one of the long line of printers who have done so much for the fame of Coalport. One thought of those printers who struck transfer after transfer of the Willow Pattern a full ten years before the Willow Pattern was being printed in the potteries. Incidentally, Mr. Ellis was famous in his younger years for his skill in crossing the Severn twice a day in a coracle, for he lived in Jackfield. No doubt there were potters in Uriconium who crossed the Severn in that ancient British craft.

Our tour of the works was rounded off by a walk through the finished warehouses where under the guidance of Mr. Lyth, until recently the company's director of sales, we

*Mr. Frederick H. Ellis, China Printer, holding print taken from original " Willow "*
*engraving.   Mr. Ellis joined the firm in 1896*

were able to see stocks of all the patterns which are illustrated in colour in this book. Times have changed in the last quarter of a century and it is seldom that Coalport are asked to supply the exceedingly rich and heavily gilt Service Plates of which they produced such large quantities between the two world wars. To-day's costs make such items more than a mere luxury.

A few more facts remain to bring this history up to date. The company's board of directors has undergone several recent changes and Mr. Stanley Harrison's colleagues now number four. Of these Mr. Eardley is, as already mentioned, responsible for general management. Mr. A. C. Lyth, who has retired to the great regret of his co-directors, had completed fifty years at the Crescent factory. His position as director of sales has been filled by Mr. Enoch Boulton who comes to Coalport not entirely unknown to many of the firm's officials. A " Potteries " man, he was closely associated with the chairman during the recent war when Mr. Harrison was commanding officer of a local battalion of the Home Guard and Mr. Boulton was its adjutant. The two other members of the board are Mrs. Stanley Harrison, the Chairman's wife, and Mr. J. Dutton, the company's secretary, who has a very important role in guiding the finances of the firm in a sound direction and in controlling office administration—no light responsibilities in these days of restrictions and the demands of government departments for all manner of figures and statistics.

The chairman's father, Mr. Sydney T. Harrison, is now, at the age of eighty, enjoying a well-earned retirement at Bournemouth. In addition to having played an important part in the rebuilding of this oldest of English china

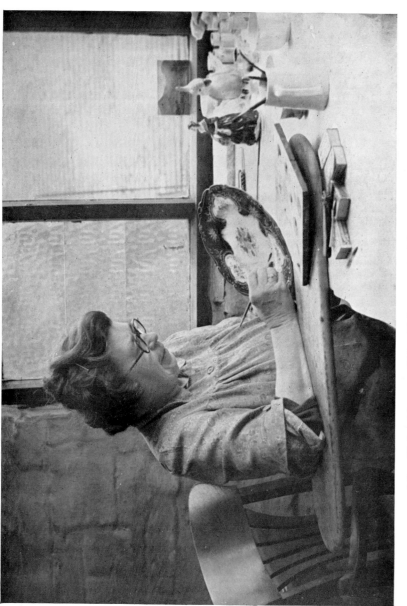

*Miss Violet Moreton, China Paintress, who joined the firm in 1898*

businesses, he devoted a great part of his time and energy, not so many years ago, to the establishment of a very different type of institution, the Cripples' Orthopædic Hospital at Hartshill in Stoke-on-Trent. Much of the success of this fine and deserving hospital is due to the untiring energy and personal attention which he gave to it in its early stages.

Among modern amenities added to the works is the extremely attractive canteen which was built in wartime and is decorated with a series of mural paintings from the hands of various members of the staff. One recalls Muss who painted landscapes for Coalport china a century and a half ago and afterwards went to London to become a fashionable landscape-painter. It would be pleasant to foresee such a career for one of the painters or paintresses at the Crescent Works, but china remains agreeably and obstinately old fashioned in its designs and may we long be spared the fashionable landscape of the moment on our plates or tea-pots !

A sound enterprise, however, can never stand still and the present owners of Coalport, while conscious of the great heritage handed down to them through two centuries, are planning for the future years. We asked the present Chairman of the company for his views on its future policy and here they are :

Some of our best patterns, including those illustrated in this book, are likely to be in production almost *ad infinitum*. Having stood the test of popularity for many years, it is unlikely that a sudden end is planned for them as yet.

New patterns will constantly be produced, since Coalport possesses a store of copper engravings probably unequalled by any other china factory, and from these will be built up from

*Mr. Leonard R. Barber, China Caster.   He joined the firm in 1900*

time to time, attractive designs enriched by the colours in vogue at the time, and produced at a price to suit the well-worn pocket of to-day. It will always be our aim to obtain the services of the best brains available, both executive, as well as manual, in order to ensure that Coalport products for the future shall be of the highest quality, and in the tradition handed down since the days of Thomas Turner. Quality, harmony in design and dignity will never be sacrificed in order to achieve low prices; which will be maintained through the policy of planning the factory in such a way that all unnecessary work—such as the carrying of ware from one department to another several times over and inefficient methods of handling—is entirely eliminated. Every modern method as used in industry to-day is being, and will continue to be installed, as long as it does not affect the quality and breeding of the products. I would also mention that experiments in the production of coloured bodies on the renowned Sèvres Embossed shape have been satisfactorily concluded and it may not be long before Coalport China in attractive new pastel shades will be available for the lovers of tinted china.

And now a last glance backwards from the present and future into the past.

In one workshop we saw the old Caughley clock whose niche is still visible over the porch of the gamekeeper's cottage. The date under the face is 1759. How many myriads of ticks have told the time for men and women now dust, some of whose mugs and plates still survive with their Tournay sprigs that Billingsley brought from Pinxton, and Turner's Blue Coomassie and Canton, and George Hancock's rose du Barry, and Walker's maroon, and the Broseley Blue Dragon and the Indian Tree, and dearest of them all, the Willow Pattern of our own childhood.

*The willow pattern that we knew*
*In childhood, with its bridge of blue*
*Leading to unknown thoroughfares.*

THE END

*The old Caughley Clock, dated 1759, now*
*in the Flower Painting Shop at Coalport*
*Works*

# *Appendix*

FOR THE benefit of readers who cannot decipher the verse in the *Dreadful Calamity* document reproduced on page 48 :

ALAS ! alas ! the fated night,
    Of cold October's twenty third,
In seventeen hundred ninety nine,
    What cries ! what lamentations heard !
The hour nine, when from yon pile,
    Where fair porcelain takes her forms ;
Where Energy with Genius joins
    To robe her in those matchless charms ;—
A wearied band of artists rose,
    Males and females old and young,
Their toils suspend to seek repose,
    Their homes to gain they bent along.
Sabrina's stream was near to pass
    And she her frowning waves uprear'd ;
Her mist condensed to darksome haze,
    Which mock'd the light, no star appear'd
Yon boat, which o'er her bosom rides,
    Envelop'd in the heavy gloom,
Convulsive stretch'd along her side,
    To snatch the victims to their doom
Soon e'er off board the falt'ring bark,
    A monster fell ! who grasp'd the helm,
Hove from the shore the destin'd crew,
    And lo ! the dreadful overwhelm !
Swift Horror's wings o'erspread the tide,
    They sink ! they rise ! they shriek ! they cling !

Again they sink ! alarm swift flies !
  Along the shores dread clamours ring !
But O ! the blackest night preventing
  Every means to save their breath ;
Helpless—hopeless—life despairing—
  Twenty-eight sunk down in death ! !
Alas ! small time for heaven implorings—
  Quick sealed their everlasting state—
Or in misery—or in glory—
  The last tribunal will relate.
Here fold, O Muse, thy feeble wings,
  Hope where thou can'st—but not decide :
Dare not approach those hidden things,
  With Mercy—Justice—they abide.
Return with sympathetic breath,
  See yon distracted mother stands !
Three daughters lost ! to heaven she lifts
  Her streaming eyes and wringing hands.
Hark ! from those dells how deep the wailing !
  Fathers, mothers, join their moans !
Widows, orphans, friends, and lovers
  Swell the air with poignant groans !
Recluse in grief those worthy masters
  Silent drop the mournful tear :
Distress pervades surrounding hamlets,
  Sorrow weeps to every ear.
Sleepless sighing hail the morning
  Morning brings no soothing ray ;
The turbid waters not admitting
  Sight to where the bodies lay.
See them now in strict researches,
  Pierce and drag the river's bed,
Eddys, fords, and rocks imploring
  To give up their silent dead.
Now one, and now another's found,
  And rescued from the wasting waves ;
Reviving griefs attend arround,
  And pity bears them to their graves.
How great the loss of shining artists !
  How desponding in their end !
How deeply felt the gone support

Of children, fathers, mothers, friends !
O ye, bereft of earthly comfort,
   Seek it from the realms above,
God gave the life, he takes away,
   Tax not his mercy or his love :
Make him your friend by supplication,—
   Tell him your despairing grief,—
Ask the power of true submission,—
   And bag the balm of heaven's relief.
And ye who foiled the jaws of death,*
   Ye, whom that vent'ring hero saved,†
Ye, who escap'd that vengeful hour,‡
   In which your comrades were enwaved :—
Will you no ardent praises raise,
   To Him, by whose supreme controul
The elements give life or death,
   In vengeance or in mercy roll ?
Will you those just commands deride,
   Which bid you fear and love your God—
His sabbaths keep—His precepts own—
   And bend your steps to his abode ?
Will you in Satan's cause combine,
   And run in hell's destructive race ?
Will you the scorn'd and scorner join,
   And spit in tender Mercy's face ?
Forbid it reason's pleading voice.—
   Forbid all ye powers above,—
Forbid it truth's celestial ray,—
   Forbid it gratitude and love.
O let your lengthen'd hours proclaim
   The sparing mercies of your God ;
Walk humbly with him all your days—
   Revere his goodness—dread his rod.

*Thirteén men, women, and children who got safe to shore.
†Edward Parker, an excellent swimmer, fetched off two boys, who clung to the boat.
‡Several persons who used to go over at that hour but by some unseen Providence had left work at six o'clock.

EXTRACT from the Indictment connected with the Trade Union dispute, reproduced on page 70 :

## We vindicate our Proceedings on the following grounds :

FIRSTLY,—THAT UNIONS AMONGST THE OPERATIVES CAN NEVER TEND PERMANENTLY TO RAISE THE PRICE OF ANY MANUFACTURED ARTICLE.

SECONDLY,—THAT IT IS IMPOSSIBLE TO FORM ANY SOCIETY OF THIS DESCRIPTION, THAT CAN BE LASTING AND EFFICIENT.

THIRDLY,—THAT THIS PARTICULAR ESTABLISHMENT WAS THE LAST, ON WHICH SUCH AN EXPERIMENT OUGHT TO HAVE BEEN TRIED.

In the first place then,—That Unions amongst Operatives, can never tend permanently to raise prices, is answered by a self-evident proposition, amounting almost to an Axiom : viz.: That the price of Goods depends on the relative bearing of supply and demand ; for as a rise in Prices is produced by a deficiency of the supply, as compared with the demand,—so low prices are occasioned by the supply being greater than the consumption. But what would be the consequence if the Prices were raised ? *It is evident there would not be so much consumed; and consequently, a large number of Workmen thrown out of employ.* This would be a case in any species of Manufactured Goods, even of what may be termed Necessaries ;—how much greater therefore would be the falling off in the consumption of *fancy goods*, the purchase of which, depends entirely on the taste and caprice of the Public.

This resolves itself into one simple truth, that " No Operations of the Unions can increase consumption ; " and that the principal cause of low wages, arises from the excessive number of Workmen in every branch of industry.

Secondly,—That it is impossible to form any Society of this description, that can be lasting and efficient, is equally clear ; as is well observed in a very able Pamphlet on this subject, that, " The Elements of a Permanent Union do not exist among Operatives ; " differing too much in sentiment, and too jealous of one another, ever to agree long together. Besides, men depending on the daily labour of their hands, are not in a condition to dictate to their employers ; their wants being too immediate to allow them to refuse, for any length of time, employment even at a moderate remuneration. The

Union with all its " Gigantic power," will never be able to prevent this ; and, " The laws of nature will be found more imperative, than the laws of the Union."

In the third case,—That this particular Establishment was the last, on which such an experiment ought to have been made, *was the expressed opinion of those who now arrange themselves as its most bitter enemies:* neither can they deny, that they have experienced more liberty and liberality—more constant employment—and, less oppression—than every they found under any other masters. And if there is any ground of complaint, it must be laid to the extreme generosity of Mr. ROSE, in striving to find, in bad times, employment for a *surplus number of hands*, to the detriment of his own pocket, and to the injury of old workmen.

---

We hope the above will satisfy the Country, that we are not acting from selfish views, but from sound and true principles, in refusing to join a secret Society, whose whole object would not be revealed till an illegal Oath was administered, which was meant to bind to resolutions, we have too good reason for thinking, would be prejudicial to the best interests of the Country. And those few amongst us, who have been persuaded by their associates to enrol themselves Members, but who have also made a timely retreat from a Society, which they felt in cooler moments, was embracing objects incompatible with the good of the Trade, do not hesitate in declaring they feel *perfectly justified* within themselves, for having acted as they have ; justly considering they committed an error, in being hurried away by the general feeling around them ; but that it would be a two-fold error in adhering to a System, which in their consciences, they could not approve. We beg leave at the same time, to assure the Public, that notwithstanding what is said to the contrary, this Manufactory is proceeding in a satisfactory and successful manner, employing at this present time, about four hundred Persons, who are willing to serve to their utmost their present Masters, not as his " *Slaves*," but as Men, who have the right to dispose of their labour at the best price they can fairly obtain, without wishing to dictate or interfere with the internal management of the concern, which always found us employment through the most depressed period. We still rely on our Employers only for justice—and they on us for exertion.

# EARLY BACKSTAMPS
## CAUGHLEY MARKS

SALOPIAN

or                    *Impressed on the ware*

Salopian

TURNER.

S          S                              C

※

S o          *The S stands for Salopian*

S          Sₓ

S
XX          *Imitation of the Dresden Mark*
X

          SALOPIAN.

On this page and the next are examples of early Caughley and Coalport backstamps which may be a useful guide to the reader. Detailed explanatory notes on each mark can be found in *Marks and Monograms on European and Oriental Pottery and Porcelain* by William Chaffers (London: William Reeves (Bookseller) Ltd.)

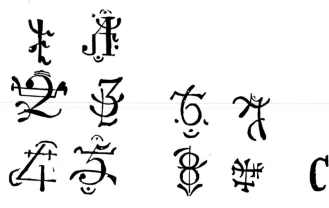

*Disguised numerals used by Turner*

## COALPORT MARKS

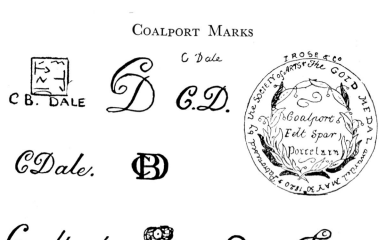

*C. B. DALE refers to Coalbrookdale*

*C, S, N on the mark on the extreme right, bottom line, refers to Caughley,*
*Swansea and Nantgarw*